JOHN MICHAEL KOFFI

REFUGE-E: THE
JOURNEY
MUCH
DESIRED

Dear Julian,

Readers are gift to writers.
And readers into write one
miracles. Thank You!

with love,
JMKoffi

Tellwell Talent
www.tellwell.ca

ISBN
978-1-77370-824-9 (Hardcover)
978-1-77370-823-2 (Paperback)
978-1-77370-825-6 (eBook)

TABLE OF CONTENTS

DEDICATION

For you, Dad and Mum, and all the parents like you;
to you, Alberto, and all refugee youth like us.

AUTHOR'S NOTE

The Syrian refugee crisis intensified in August and September of 2015. The United World College (UWC) Robert Bosch College community held a meeting on September 7, 2015, arranged by one of the students, to discuss how we could address the influx of refugees in Freiburg, Germany, where the school is located. Being a "specialist" on the matter, I shared my story along with a poem I had written while in Swaziland. The present work was inspired by the community members' encouragement and heartfelt gratitude for how I had informed or changed their perspectives on the lives of refugees. I started writing this book while on my trip back to school from winter break on January 6, 2016.

I have written this book primarily to share my story. It is by no means a comprehensive account, for there is much more to it than can be expressed in words.

Note that a few names have been altered to conceal their identities.

I hope *Refuge-e: The Journey Much Desired* can instill a sense of responsibility in those who are capable of making a difference in the lives of others, especially the lives of the refugee youth, and that it gives hope to those who need it, no matter the countless obstacles the world continues to put in our way.

With love,

JMK

PROLOGUE:

BLUE HOUR

I grew up with two loving parents and an extended family; I played with cousins and friends; and I wandered in the hills and valleys. I knew affection and attachment, and I was oblivious to the harsh realities of life.

When I was a toddler, I was fascinated by the rain: I loved playing in it and sleeping as it fell outside. While family and friends meant safety and the hills and valleys meant a taste of freedom, rain meant escape from all that haunted my innocence. The thunderstorms' magical power chased away the all-too-usual sounds of bombs and bullets. Magnificent lightning drew my attention away from where the next flames might appear, and the smell of falling raindrops overshadowed the strong stench of rotting bodies.

Every time I hear the rain, I close my eyes and think of home. It is never quite the same. I am hailed by the long-gone enchanted sounds of raindrops on our iron sheet–roofed houses. I hear distant voices of mothers competing with the thunderstorms, sometimes excitedly asking us, "Come inside. Get out of the rain." At other times, coldly: "Put a bucket under the leakage or the house will be all awash!" And still other times, pathetically: "Collect as much water as you can, you fool! You won't need to go down to the stream and die like your … *brother? Sister? Cousin?*" I see the darkness that accompanies the heavy rainfalls that used to set me free from all sorts of thoughts—thoughts of my friends, with whom we played and who would disappear the next day like dreams upon waking; of the dreadful sight of those poor, innocent souls groaning after torture or rape; of threats to my family and to my friends' families.

I would like to think those days are gone. Sadly, I still see them. Sometimes back in the past where they belong, other times as present memories. Often in the future. The more I run the more quickly I bump into them, these bittersweet reminders of the future that I long to see and the future that lies far in the past.

For eight years now, there have been no heavy rains to set me free from myself and my thoughts. Thoughts about the truths twisted by the media; the pitiful images and conditions of those who, like me, are on the run after torture and rape; the threats to my family, to millions of other families, to the future; the young hunting for opportunities to better the future.

It is July 12, 2017, a little after five o'clock in the afternoon. I am sitting on top of artificial rocks at the bank of the

Pegnitz river, close to Ebenseesteg in Nuremberg, Germany. It is raining, and the clouds seem pregnant as they eagerly hinder the sunrays from trespassing their colonies. I wish I was small, the little fella who ran on top of hills and at the bottom of valleys, playing with the droplets decelerated by tree leaves in the *safe* parts of the forests. But I can't! I am alone and lonely. Do I just go to sleep, with a troubled mind and restless spirit?

I am holding a fifth-generation iPhone in my hands. Some say it is made from conflict minerals. I often wonder if they even know where the Democratic Republic of Congo is! At least with this iPhone I can play "Futa Machozi" ("Wipe Tears")—one of my songs.

I am trying hard to listen to all the sounds around me. My song; the harmony of the turbulent water trying so hard to gulp some air as it flows surely downstream; the soft tree leaves hissing as the branches tending them dance slowly and freely to the rhythm of the calm breeze. The birds chirping sad and happy melodies in the background. The railroads in the distance that cannot resist the heavy weight of the periodic trains. The sounds of moving aircraft up high, far beyond where I can see them.

The Canadian embassy has denied me a study permit. I have reapplied, but there is little hope. I am stuck in Nuremberg, Hitler's favorite city, and I have been in Germany for one year, ten months and twenty-one days. I have successfully completed the International Baccalaureate Diploma Program and graduated from UWC Robert Bosch College as one of its most reputable students. I have exceeded my own expectations—that much I know. But who cares?

I am a refugee, and that is all that matters.

CHAPTER 1:

DARK

Dzaleka Refugee Camp, formerly known as Zaleka, is a transformed political prison notorious for being the worst prison to ever have existed in Malawi. The stories tell that when prisoners were brought here they were unlikely to survive. The camp is located on a high plateau in the Dowa Highlands, about fifty kilometers northeast of Lilongwe, the capital city of Malawi. Its elevation and flatness mean brutally cold winters and extremely dry, windy summers bitterly devoid of rain. The prison guards of Zaleka enjoyed exposing prisoners to the extreme cold and, as accounts went, would often leave a prisoner completely naked outside overnight. A prisoner who survived the cold would be set free in the following days, having paid the harshest penalty one could ever get for crime: nature's cruelty. Yet most who were exposed to the unforgiving cold never saw the sunrise again. It was in this place that the Malawian government decided to set up a refugee camp.

During the late 1980s and throughout the 1990s, the upheavals that led to the terrors of the Rwandan Genocide and the vicious civil war in Burundi caused many citizens from the two countries to flee, most of them sticking close to their homelands in the northwestern part of Tanzania, the eastern part of the Democratic Republic of the Congo, and southern Uganda. A significant number of those in Tanzania moved farther south into Malawi and Mozambique.

These refugees were first kept in Luwani Refugee Camp in the Southern Region of Malawi, which was opened to host Mozambican refugees during the Mozambican Civil War (1977–92). When it was closed in 2007, the multitudes who lived there, mainly from the Great Lakes and the Horn of Africa, were moved into Dzaleka Refugee Camp. In addition to witnessing the horrors of Rwanda and Burundi, the unstable Great Lakes region, whose politics are so synonymous with tragedy, also saw the first and second Congo Wars. These were mostly instigated by the Congolese richesse, the falling dictatorship of Mobutu and the rise of the Kabila dynasty, the post-genocide Rwandan government, and rebel groups of all kinds. They were driven by ethnic tensions, especially in the provinces of North and South Kivu. Thus, countless more entered refugee camps all over Africa, including Dzaleka Refugee Camp.

By the time my family arrived in Dzaleka, the camp was estimated to hold more than eleven thousand refugees, making it one of the largest refugee camps in southern Africa. Many Westerners today equate Africa with misery, war, and starvation—the "dark continent," as its moniker states. In addition to the Burundian, Rwandan, and Congolese refugees, there were many Somalians, Ethiopians, and other minority groups from other parts of Africa. We set foot in the camp in September 2009, joining other innocent souls who had been deprived of their dignity by all sorts of greedy games and manmade calamities.

The camp was windy. Blades of grass flew from roof to roof, following the whirling wind that blew both the cold, dry, dusty air and the absolute uncertainty of what tomorrow might look like for the camp's inhabitants. I had never experienced that kind of wind, dust, and despair. There was no sign of rain whatsoever.

We had just arrived, and like everyone, we had no one. Nonetheless, we had to adapt—to come to terms with the overflowing sorrow and the desolate desperation that had seized us ever since we left the African Great Lakes Region. We had fled from bombs and bullets and traveled what felt like a million miles to find comfort and safety, but every step seemed to desert faith and push away hope. The calmness and tranquility that at times embraced our troubled journey competed with an enormous sorrow, one that could only be read and interpreted by the Almighty.

We had all been wounded: physically, mentally, emotionally. Spirituality was our only escape, and only so for a small segment of the family. A few of us had given up already. After all, a God who did not keep the malicious fire from burning all your belongings, all your properties, and all you owned; who had not prevented death, rape, and torture in the family; who let you flee from your home, culture, and traditions, your landscapes, hills, and valleys—who and where was he? I imagine that was the core question for some, although others could have responded simply that he is the God who allowed you to survive all that and to breath Malawian air, that even though that air is full of dust and dejection, you should praise the one who allowed it to run through your lungs and veins. The mere fact that your veins did not spill their contents is a miracle that should be celebrated!

Seemingly settled bodies still contained unsettled minds, and like all the people we encountered there, we soon found in resettlement a new utopian hope. At least there was hope. A drop in the ocean.

There were no books or boots. Blue band was a long-forgotten history. We just had to survive.

In the following days, I started feeling life there. I became increasingly unsettled by seeing people who seemed happy; in retrospect, happiness had fled my mind at the time. I sat, wretchedly watching the sun set and the darkness swiftly creep in day after day, wondering what destiny held in store. I was not happy, but I had *hope*. Hope kept me going.

The first dark days of our arrival in Malawi hastened by, and soon people—especially those who had been there for years—slowly started to come into our lives. Friendly people, curious people, cynics. Some came to sympathize, others to introduce us to the new life, this new heavenly Hell we had just landed in. I soon came to understand that no man is an island and that though mountains can never meet, people can. All it takes is time.

My father found some long-lost friends while I wandered quietly in different corners of Dzaleka trying to familiarize myself with the place; I was a curiously disconsolate spirit reminiscing on friends I had lost back home through flight, kidnapping, or death, wondering if I would ever gain any new comrades. There were a few, just two or three, but they were there, some of whom my father had assisted in their hour of need when he was still a person and not a refugee. When you act kindly, you find kindness ahead in your journey. Even thousands of kilometers from their homelands, some people still recognized the values they had grown up embracing, values that transcended wars and divisions. Care, respect, assisting those in *need* while disregarding your own *neediness*—all these values mark many cultures and traditions in Africa. We were helped with getting shelter: a dilapidated compound in "Blantyre" that would soon become our home after my brothers and I sweat blood to reconstruct the place and build new structures. The different sections of Dzaleka were named after major cities, towns, or places from across the country like Zomba and Blantyre in the southern part of Malawi or Kawale in Lilongwe. Finding this compound in Blantyre was a step in the right direction, even though it was incredibly difficult to start a new life there as new arrivals who had nothing.

It was in those days that my father wandered all over the camp and its surroundings trying to find the grass that we could use to thatch the roofs, while my brothers and I dug the soil and made mud bricks. Large families, however burdensome they are in these times of trouble, can also be beneficial. Our coordinated efforts helped us rebuild the site that we had stumbled upon. We reconstructed the ruins, ensuring that my father and mother had a room to themselves, my two sisters another, and that we had a living room between the two bedrooms. We also reconstructed another adjacent ruin to create two rooms shared between my two brothers and me. Soon we built a pit latrine on the ditch we had dug for the soil used to make bricks; next to it, we constructed an improvised enclosure for showering with crushed stones on the floor to make sure that water would drain, preventing the water accumulation that most likely would have attracted mosquitoes and malaria. A few months later, after hustling for survival, we would connect my parents and sisters' house to ours with a small room in which we sold groceries; we created a kitchen area right in front of our house adjacent to the room, connecting this building with another poorly but surely improvised room for raising chickens. All these structures connected so well that the whole place became a closed compound—a safe haven with maximum security.

My father was the engineering genius behind this whole masterpiece, telling us what to do and how to do it. I often wondered what the man could not do!

Besides the luck of having a place to lay our heads amid the cold, dust, and despair of Dzaleka, the effort to rec-create our plot and make it livable ensured that the whole family had something to look forward to. This significantly dammed the constant surge of thoughts on what we had lost, who we had lost, and the attributes of our new Hell. It helped heal the wounds we had endured while fleeing. Even if my mother had no salt for food and my sisters no soap to bathe with, the satisfaction and joy of having a place we could call home magnified the hope that tomorrow would be better. Making bricks was a valuable skill for my brothers and me to learn, and later we would make thousands of them for money and survival.

Soon, my brothers and I would go throughout the camp looking for dead or abandoned radio batteries. We aligned them together to make a long chain that would produce enough voltage to power the small bulbs on the circuit boards of dysfunctional torches that were also thrown in the garbage pits. We spent hours foraging for these materials because we realized that this was the main method of lighting the grass-thatched dwellings in the camp; it was also the cheapest since we had no money for paraffin lamps. It was safe because only a few individuals in Dzaleka had legal electricity. Those who were privileged enough to have power distributed it to their immediate neighbors, especially if they were of the same nationality, and the cables and wires were dangerously and inexpertly connected such that if one house were to blow up, the whole camp would burn to ashes. ESCOM, the electricity company in Malawi, had warned the camp residents about this, but it never hindered people from doing the installations in the middle of the night: you would sleep and discover the next day that your neighbor had electricity, out of the blue! We had not reached that level of friendship with our neighbors, so for us physics worked its magic and we lived on sustainably.

One of the friends my father had encountered was a teacher at Umodzi Katubza Full Primary School

(UKFPS). Through him, we heard about the changing educational system in Malawi and that the new school term would start much earlier than usual. The Malawian government was adopting the September–July academic calendar and discarding the previous one (January–December). Registration for the new refugee students was taking place at UKFPS. The Jesuit Refugee Service (JRS) sought to ensure every child's basic human right to education by building the UKFPS in Dzaleka Refugee Camp; the school served more than 2,800 refugee and Malawian children at the time, although it was mainly intended for the former. I looked forward to joining them.

I had finished sixth grade when we left my homeland. Despite the bombs and bullets that disrupted my everyday learning environment, education meant the world to me.

My father, too, wanted to see me get educated. And so it was on one of those sorrowful, stressful November days that we went to enroll. There was no test in place to assess the capacities of prospective learners and assign them to appropriate grades. The administration was reluctant to place children in either Grade 7 or Grade 8. Malawi follows the 5-3-2-2 education system, where Grades 7 and 8 are the two final years of primary school. I had completed Grade 6 and had to be in Grade 7. This was my obstinate mentality.

"He does not speak English," the teacher at the registration table told my father. "He comes directly from a French educational system, one that is very different from here, and without any English we cannot guarantee what kind of pupil he will be. Especially in Grade 7."

My father listened carefully to the semifluent English of the Malawian teacher, and then to the fluent Swahili of the translator, who made sure not to miss any word said by either of the two parties. My father knew neither how to react nor how to reply. Gathering all his calmness, he told the interpreter: "I know my child. He has always been the best. You just have to give him a chance."

The more I listened to their conversation, the greater the flood of tears that gathered in my eyes, threatening to erode the enthusiasm I had come with. I was not used to crying out of emotion, but school was something I had always cared about.

"Mr. … we are also striving for equality here. Your kid is just like the rest."

"But, can't you, just …"

"Well, the only thing we can do is enroll him in the sixth grade, then after a while, looking at his progress, we will decide whether he is fit for the seventh grade or not. Please leave his name here."

"What about …"

"Mr. Koffi, you are wasting other people's time here." The teacher did not allow my father to express his opinion on my case. His attention instantly drifted from my father. "Next, please!" he said in a harsh, agitated tone.

Strong and strange emotions overpowered me. Seeing my father intimidated once again and seeing the educational progress I aspired to refused, I cried, feeling angry and betrayed. I knew the world still rotated on its slanted axis, but the flames of the world inside me were constantly weakening. Flickering. Ever since we started our journey as refugees, my burning desire to exist had subsided day by day; the education on its own seemed as useless as life itself, contradicting the *hope* I lived with.

"Papa, I don't want to go to school anymore," I murmured, weakly and wearily. "I don't want to repeat Grade 6. I don't want to be taught by … such people." I couldn't find the appropriate adjective to describe the teacher's personality I had just witnessed; my building anger subjugated the person inside me. Emotions incapacitated my ability to speak.

"My son, education is your only way out of this refugee life, the journey that we started a few months ago." My father probably overlooked the crucial fact that he was speaking to a twelve-year-old filled with anger, agitation, and disappointment. Nonetheless, he continued: "Your mother and I are aging and your siblings are not very capable, after all that has happened. Keep in mind that you are at least lucky to be offered to repeat one class. Just one class. Others are either taken three classes back or not offered schooling at all."

At this point, he paused and quietly examined me. I was still crying and paying a little attention to him. Then he said the most important words a father can tell his son: "Focus on your studies. Trust God and your heart. That's the least you can do."

My father's teacher friend had seen my anguish and discouragement, to the point of me not wanting to attend school at all. He pressed on, insisting to the headmaster that I should indeed be enrolled into Grade 7, and it finally worked. I began lessons in early December 2009. This was also when I started to explore my faith.

Sometimes I think there is something about faith that will never cease to be arguable. God created man—man created God. Christianity and other religions do not help in bringing clarity but bring more confusion instead. In the early days of my childhood, I always got punished for everything related to the church: not attending, making noise, sleeping, forgetting what I heard, and so on. Church was this holy place where I had to be at least once a week or more. I grew up respecting the church. Although sometimes God held a lesser place than the church did, I grew up loving God the Most High. Whether he created me or was himself created by generations of forefathers before me I did not know, and I did not care so long as I lived to pray, praise, and be at peace with the world and with myself.

Growing up in a devout Catholic family, I had many questions. Thinking about the creation of God, I wondered if my distant forefathers were white. Jesus was white, at least according to the images I was exposed to as a child. The early months of 2010 were the perfect period for me to explore more of these beliefs through the history that I learned in school and my new commitments in church in Dzaleka. But these questions never left me!

"The missionaries had brought Christianity to Sub-Saharan Africa," I learned in my early lessons of social studies at UKFPS. "Dr. David Livingstone *blah blah blah blah* ... and he got lost and could not go back," Mr. Bondondo had once said in class, on one of the few days he was sober enough to teach coherently. He drank *kachasu*, a locally brewed spirit that is almost 100 percent alcohol. We had seen him peeing in his pants and uttering innumerable insults a number of times after drinking a few shots, as he staggered on his way home to one of the villages near the camp. Each time he stood in front of us to teach, I wondered whether he was in a state for teaching and whether he would disgrace himself yet again after school.

I amused myself with the thought that the precolonial and colonial history he taught in social sciences matched his character perfectly, though sometimes I wondered if the stories made sense. Who wrote them, anyway? These stories always reminded me some of the folktales my grandma used to tell my cousins and me back in the day. Like Grandma, remarkably, Mr. Bondondo knew how to tell stories about the evolution of events. I always listened to him with enthusiasm because whenever he started teaching African history—almost always written by some old white man—I closed my eyes and pictured my grandmother, whose image had sadly started to slowly fade from my small brain, leaving only an evening silhouette of her cheerful face. Then it felt as if she were the one narrating the story. After all, she had lived through some of the periods that Mr. Bondondo revealed to us, and unlike the history of colonization told from the colonizer's point of view, I had learned better from the experiential genius of Grandma. Later, after class, if melancholy had not taken the better part of me and forced me to doze off reminiscing while the stories told in class bored me to death, I would sit down and muse over some of my grandma's truer legends. One that persisted was about *Fisi*—The Great Hyenas—a folktale that for some reason managed to loiter around various regions of my brain during and after each one of Mr. Bondondo's classes.

"Shall I tell the story?" my grandma would shout.

"Tell, tell, tell, Grandma!" My cousins and I would answer in unison, and then she would start while we listened very carefully.

"A long time ago—a very, very, very long time ago— there were packs of hyenas who felt very enlightened. They fought each other, formed friendships, developed similar ways of living, established common codes of conduct, and decided that they were the best in everything that they did. Little did they know that in the region they inhabited were also dragons, lions, leopards, and all other sorts of carnivores. The abominable carnivores. They knew about these carnivores, but they thought every other creature that breathed air like them, even if they made different sounds, ran differently, or even lived differently, was there to serve them. Carnivores hunted, ate a little bit of their prey, and then left the most essential parts for their beloved, unknown friends—the Great Hyenas. Knowing that every other animal, especially the meat eaters, lived to serve them, the Great Hyenas had a strong sense of superiority that helped them to feel even more united and strong.

"Over time, there were a series of unprecedented events: some favored them and some did not. For example, the scarcity of rain caused the wretched ruminants to sacrifice themselves to the wellbeing of *Fisi*, the Mighty. As the sun shone brightly (though not too hot for the powerful hyenas, for in fact they were in the far north where the cold persisted), the ruminants scattered themselves in the dark, murky jungles or the tall, ugly, brown grass of the savannas and lay down on the ground, dead, waiting to be ingested. Or they decided to cluster in some specific abominable habitats where slowly, one by one, they would let their souls diffuse out of their flesh, offering the magnificent *Fisi* a treasure hunt that led them to their unconscious, good-natured pals waiting to be devoured. Sometimes the *Fisi* found them still fresh, before decomposition could produce its alluring smell, but the *Fisi* delighted in devouring them anyway. After all, it took a lot of courage, fondness, and devotion for these ruminants to simply lie around and sacrifice themselves to the Hyenas—the eminent.

"Sometimes, well, the abominable carnivorous friends consumed a bit of these ignorant herbivores, but so long as they left some chewy bony skeletons with a bit of some pleasant, tasty, rotting ligaments, it didn't really matter. Anyhow, the distinguished Hyena Union later realized, through their enlightenment, that there were some miserably unenlightened goats out in the woods who suffered a lot of predation—although it ended up benefiting them. Weirdly enough, the goats ate each other, something that went against the divine guidance of the Great Hyenas. Besides, the knowledgeable *Fisi* had long recognized that the backward savanna inhabitants possessed more than they fathomed or needed. They decided to intervene: first sniffing out and locating the goats, then mingling with them, mostly luring them by exchanging the transformed leftovers of the yummy bones they had crunched on before for some sympathetic members of the goat families, always disguising themselves in some wolf-like raiment they had somehow managed to secure through their enlightenment. Eventually, they ended up forcefully befriending the goats, and God knows what happened to them thereafter! The Great Hyenas shared their enlightenment, with a significant emphasis on how goats should live for them not to be preyed upon. The beloved *Fisi*, the cunning predators that tried to prey on the other players in the industry, ruled the goats, always emphasizing how the goats should never be preyed upon! And the hyenas and goats lived happily ever after, until 'ever after' ended—that is the end of part one. Still there?"

A few would answer, if any were still awake!

Sometimes I would frown at my aging, beloved grandmother and question her about what she meant by "happily ever after," but she was always quick to silence me. "You don't ask such questions," she would say hastily. "If you ask, the hyenas are going to come for you. They will make you their friend because you are becoming enlightened." Something felt odd here, but as a kid I could almost picture them laughing at the corner of my little brain, laughing so loudly that the thought on its own scared me. At night, my mother would come to take me home from my grandmother's, because I had to sleep. Then my grandmother would sit down on her mat and suck the last drops of the traditional beer out of her calabash, contemplating the other stories she would tell us the day after.

My education at UKFPS proceeded normally. Or as if everything were normal. We did not have school uniforms except for shared grief and sorrow, and this often transported me back to my previous life when I used to wake up and choose between shorts or shirts of similar colors and fabrics to wear for school. I missed those days so badly! But, thank God, at least I was now in school.

Now I had to learn and memorize things. That was what counted, especially now that my father's teacher friend had made sure that I started directly in Grade 7—I had to prove that I was capable. I had to memorize things I did not fully understand even though I had buried myself in any English-for-beginners book I came across. I always knew that the next day would be better, and that the only way there was through education. I had to follow Mr. Bondondo's *blah blah blahs* wholeheartedly.

"Then Henry Morton Stanley came to search for Dr. David Livingstone, and *blah blah blah blah.* …" He would draw links to the foreign names that we had to commit to memory. "Then came the Catholic missionaries. The white fathers were first, *blah blah blah.* … We had the … *Prespteriba-, Presbylat-, prestribylat-* … Presbyterians follow, *blah blah blah* …"

It was too much to take in sometimes, but I had to know all of this. Knowing all these tales about religion itself, I found it particularly fascinating how I had grown up as a God-fearing lad, had been baptized, had taken my first communion and even my confirmation, but had never known the history behind all that I believed. All that I believe. *Christianize me, if you may, but don't try to Europeanize me.* I happened to contemplate on that sometime, although I was not sure when, or how, or why.

It had been a little more than four months since we started breathing the dusty Malawian air. I was getting used to the place, making one friend at a time. The *phala*, a form of porridge that the school provided during breaks, had slowly started to restore roundness to my cheeks. I enjoyed it and delighted in seeing how the refugee kids fought for it, probably because that was mostly what we had to keep on living, to keep on pushing through life. The provision of porridge was a governmental initiative, in collaboration with JRS, to sustain the health of refugee children and motivate more of us to come to school. No wonder, then, that some came just for that! There were also those who we teased for having a refrigerator in their mouths: they could take a half-liter cup and swallow it within a minute while the rest of us tried to cool ours down, and even though each pupil was supposed to receive just one cup, they often jumped back into the commotion of those who had not yet had any to get more porridge. Often, the *phala* never reached the seventh and eighth grades because they started serving lower grades first and some students took much more than their share. To me, it was always a constant reminder of how hungry we were, sleeping and studying on empty stomachs while trying to get our brains to memorize Mr. Bondondo and the others' nonsense. My favorite teacher was Mr. Phiri Sr., who taught agriculture (Mr. Phiri Jr. taught science and technology). He would observe you carefully while you feebly dozed off and would continue speaking, but when you least expected it he would come from behind you and deliver a good blow on your back! It didn't matter whether he used his hand or a stick or a book; whatever he used, it was always painful and loud accompanied by a bang or an explosive sound! I liked him because he was never able to pronounce the word "characteristic." While teaching, you would hear him say, "The soil's *cha-ra-ka-ra-ri-stics* ... the *charakararistixs* of a well-pruned plant ..." and so on. It was always funny, given his fast way of speaking, the gaps between his premolars, and the fact that he was both old and small—a combination of different amusing "*karakararistics*."

In any case, during the time of Mr. Bondondo's stories, which somehow explained the source of our ideologies, I sought solace in church. I loved church! Dzaleka had two major Catholic communities: Bikira Maria Utarasamanywe Icyaha, in which the Rwandans and Burundians predominated, and St. Stevens, which was mainly Congolese. Not that the camp was overpopulated by Roman Catholics—religion is always surrounded by misunderstandings and controversy, and that was how the two parts were formed over time. My family, like many others, had found its place in the former community because St. Stevens seemed immersed in more controversial viewpoints. My father has always been a wonderful analyst; he told us to go to Bikira Maria Utarasamanywe Icyaha, and we complied.

It was in February, 2010 that I joined the children's choir, Dominiko Savio, and soon after I started playing keyboard for them. I had owned a keyboard back home before we fled. The bad thing about being a refugee, besides losing or leaving loved ones, is that refugees can't move around with anything. You were safe if you were empty handed, and if you were not, there were professionals to help you empty your hands—with or without your cooperation. I had experience with both options but truly hated the latter. At least with the former, you had someone else to blame for the continued evolution of your tragedies, unlike when you willingly decided to forsake all the belongings that you valued—almost like forsaking your own life. It seemed like assisted suicide—who you would blame when you safely arrived in Hell or Heaven? I never had a chance to flee with my keyboard. It was too large to carry around, hence too risky.

Joining the choir was a light springing from this dark tunnel, a timely illumination. For the first time since we left my home country, I did not feel lonely. I started surrounding myself with peers and adults who were drawn to my musical talents. We had singing rehearsals every Tuesday from 3 p.m. to 5 p.m., and on Saturdays from 2 p.m. to 4 p.m. Like many other boys, we came an hour or so before choir practice to play soccer. This turned into a new hobby, but sometimes I just sat down and watched while others played. I would occasionally witness how they offended each other, voluntarily or not. This normally led to shouts, which led to insults, which would almost lead to fights unless an adult appeared.

"Take time to observe and analyze," my father had said back in the day, "and match the actions with the verbal expressions. That is how you can truly know who a friend might be. And remember our ancestors used to say, 'Show me your friends, and I will tell who you are.' The world around us is in shambles, my son, but you will have a future only if you surround yourself with the right people." He always ended with sentences that contained ifs and conditionals that took me an eternity to comprehend. Some lingered long enough to be understood only later, in my mid-teens.

Although it was through school that I met Alberto, our friendship grew more from being neighbors and singing in the choir. I was in Grade 7 and he was in Grade 6, but in the choir we were equals. He seemed cool–he was cool. He would play soccer with the rest of the boys, careful enough not to make a misplay or offend anyone, and when some minor disagreement was born he would step in between the aggrieved parties to settle the case. His impression was that of an honest boy, one who would certainly turn out to be a proper friend. Being neighbors allowed us to communicate and go to church together, whether on weekdays for rehearsals or on Sundays for the actual service. His voice stood out among the whole children's choir. Unlike the other boys and me, he did not force his singing voice. It was much more natural, flowing from deep within with such an intensity that it entertained while communicating the divine message. I always wondered how he managed to do that. I had never sung in a choir before, though I had written and played my own childhood—or childish—songs. The ones my father exaggeratedly nodded to, saying they would get me far, whenever I implored his *sagesse*.

I soon started learning a few things about Alberto. His family had arrived in Dzaleka when he was very little. He was "too miniature in body and brain size to remember!" or so he said. He lived with his mother, brother, and stepfather. I never asked about his birth father. Maybe Alberto's father was a government soldier back in our crumbling home country. Perhaps he was a rebel in one of the groups that dutifully opposed, or pretended to oppose, both the government and the presence of the United Nations peacekeeping missions. (The soldiers from the Mission de l'Organization des Nations Unies en République Démocratique du Congo [MONUC], I had heard, were the ones who made it possible for the mineral businesses to go on. They traded bombs and bullets for coltan, diamonds, and precious stones in general that had no use to the Congolese people, thereby allowing the militants like Congrès National pour la Défense du Peuple [CNDP] and Forces Démocratique de Libération du Rwanda [FDLR], who wanted to liberate our country from evil leaders, to function well. I was still too much of a knucklehead to comprehend these issues. What was CNDP or FDLR anyway? Just a bunch of letters.) Maybe he had been burned in his house and never managed to escape the escalating malice of ethnic conflicts tied to the military and political crises excitedly watched by the whole world. I had all these theories but never dared to ask him! I was afraid of his likely reaction, for I knew some outbursts could happen from curious minds trying to find out more than they could know. I hated emotional outbursts from people when they talked, willingly or not, about their problems.

Alberto's mother preferred his older brother to him, possibly because his brother was better looking and a little bit antisocial. Alberto was always searching for answers to these unending puzzles of life, too. Sometimes, I sensed his quest for emotional support.

"We are both the last born," he told me one day, "but our places in the family are different."

"Why do you think so?" I asked dutifully.

"Well, you have more brothers and sisters, and both a mother and a father"

"So?" this was an earnest query. I did not see the point here. And this was a chat between two twelve-year-old boys.

"You have more love than I do."

"Maybe you are right. Maybe you are wrong. How would you measure love?"

"Nobody shouts at you. Nobody refuses to give you food if there is any. Nobody tells you that you are stupid even when you get the second-best position in class, even though they have never stepped into Grade 1."

"Hmmm. Alberto …"

I sensed some manly, swallowed sorrow that was rarely expressed. Emotions. I guess that was the chemistry of bonding taking place. Pity arose in me, but I did not want to show any signs of it. I just didn't feel like it, partly because for bonding to take place two things must often be the exact opposite, and partly because we were in the early days of our ever-growing brotherhood. This conversation made me understand why he spent most of his time away from home, with friends. Different types of friends.

Dzaleka had many talented young people. Most of them specialized in dancing, and there were often competitions or shows that any young adult capable of paying fifty kwacha or more could hardly miss. Among these were the "Cash Money," the "Super Crew," and the "G-Unit." All of them had adapted their names from some singer or dancer group in the United States. They dressed differently: long, fake silver or gold chains on top of oversized T-shirts and hoodies, baggy jeans whose waistbands lay below the buttocks, and so on. They stayed mostly in their groups. In their midst were "Mary Jane" and girls, the ultimate source of fun. They all pursued fame, even if it meant a deliberate obliviousness to the culture, traditions, and values their parents—if they still had them at that point—had taught them. It wasn't uncommon for them to hear a lot of disapproval from the older generation.

Alberto used to hang out with some of these groups, more often than one would have expected of him. He wasn't a dancer like they were. He didn't want fame. He dressed purely, like an altar boy, for it was who he was in our inconsolable, despairing refugee community. At least that was what I observed. I wondered why he invested so much time in them. Didn't he have books and a Bible? I had been told that life could not be life without the constant seeking of extensive knowledge complemented by divine presence and inspiration, that books and the Bible both contained extensive knowledge, divine presence, and inspiration, and that you either stuck to these or to the likes of Cash Money and G-Unit. You could not serve or slave for both kings. Alberto seemed to manage at first when I met him, but soon he started to miss choir practices, carried away by the activities of the other groups. Inexplicable activities, mostly.

"We were watching movies, and I forgot," he would tell me, one of his most frequent excuses.

"What kind of movies?" I would ask reproachfully. Had it been "a movie" or at least some titled movie series, it would have been fine; but the term "movie" had an under-tone. The more we interacted, the more I sensed some emotions involved. Some feelings or even a strong sensa-tion associated with "movies." An undertone of something erotic. Worse, I feared mental corruption and sin. I had a lot of fears. But that was just me, a little more judgmental and apprehensive.

"Movies, you know!" would come the far-fetched answer. Not convincing or enlightening in any way!

"Which movies?" They didn't have titles and were many, like short segmented clips—six-, ten-, perhaps thirty-minute-long clips. That was my problem.

"Come on, get over it. I won't forget again!" That calm nature and tranquil smile could transcend my forced, or rather enforced, unjustified anger. Then we could change the topic.

But soon the forgetfulness became a habit. Alberto dropped out of the choir. He stopped reading in church and serving in mass. I soon found myself obliged to find "the lost sheep," as our choir master called him. I did not judge the curves life brought his way, but I was concerned. Days and weeks passed, and many people started to take notice. Once praised by my father and other elders for his activeness in church, Alberto had started some murmurs with his apparent truancy. Before I knew it, I was getting remarks:

> "Get your friend back to church …"
> "Have you been with Alberto lately?"
> "Are you still hooked up with your friend?"

Sometimes these rhetorical questions were not too explicit, but I knew they were telling me: "You better stop being friends with this guy." I had my uncertainties, but I did not allow them to take over the better part of me.

"Do you ever judge me?" Alberto once seized an opportunity to ask me. We were standing by the borehole waiting for our turns to pump and fetch water. One of the best things that the United Nations High Commissioner for Refugees (UNHCR) ever did for Dzaleka Refugee Camp was to build numerous boreholes. If the lack of sanitation were to have been combined with a lack of clean water, life would have been even more of a calamity than it already was. Boreholes were also places were young people coming to fetch water socialized, although fights often broke out due to deliberate misunderstandings about who came before whom.

As he asked me this, Alberto threw me an intent look, possibly to indicate the gravity of the question. I could tell he was very insecure. He was much more silent and hardly seen in those days, especially during daylight. He was active at night instead, like the bats back home before we fled, when we used to own proper houses and buildings. Being active at night meant being with nighttime friends too. The other friends.

"Why should I?" I asked, trying hard not to seem cynical. A lot of things were done in the night; many not-so-good things. But I let that pass.

"Because I no longer go to church with you."

"But we still spend time together, don't we?"

"Not really."

"Do you judge yourself then?"

"Not really."

"You spend most of your time with your other friends?"

"Yes. But … [pause] Not really."

"What do you mean, *not really*?" I raised my voice a little higher. His remained flat. It was evident that neither of us understood where the talk was heading. He had started it, and I had jumped in and took control like a disconcerted passenger would seize the wheel from the driver, which was not usually the case. "I wouldn't be happy to lose you," I said toward the end of the conversation.

"I couldn't imagine myself losing you too!" was all he said.

Time passed, and somehow school started to become fun. I started to engage more deeply, and not just in class. I participated in quiz competitions and won prizes as the best-performing student in different categories, especially in science and mathematics. I had built my reputation for this. I became a member of two school clubs: the Boys and Girls Future Club and the Wildlife Club. The Boys and Girls Future club was led by a Congolese refugee who taught "Life Skills" in Grade 8 classes. Naturally, the club became all about life skills. We would meet from time to time to talk about all sorts of things, and for the first time I learned about sexually transmitted diseases: HIV and AIDS, the likes of gonorrhea and syphilis, and the human papilloma virus (HPV). It was all interesting, yet little did I know I was accumulating knowledge that I was to disperse to some hopeless and helpless characters like myself soon, in a different country.

The other club, which became even more important for me, was the Wildlife Club. I fell in love with it within the very first days at the initial meetings. I had always known that I loved nature. Nature brought me joy. Two terms down the line, the club members voted me in as the chairperson. They were influenced by the patron, a Chichewa-language teacher who constantly observed my commitment and interest in the club and its activities. As part of my duties, I helped plan and decide on the activities. We learned about different natural attractions in Malawi, from Nyika National Park in Karonga, in the far northern parts of Malawi, to the Nkhotakota Game Reserve right in the center and Mwabvi Wildlife Reserve in the southernmost tip of the country. The attractions were endless! We met regularly to talk about nature, biodiversity, and conservation. Sometimes other students thought we were out of our minds. *Who wastes their time talking about living things?* And they weren't alone. Once, I was crazy enough to tell my family that I wanted to pursue zoology. As an African child in the twenty-first century, you can always anger the ancestors within your parents by talking about having a future profession other than being a medical doctor, lawyer, or engineer! It always works!

My passion for nature had lured me to join the Wildlife Club at the beginning of the year, and when I joined my hope was to visit one of Malawi's great nature reserves someday. Not only did the dream come true, but as the chairperson of the club I also got to participate in the decision of where we would go. My friends wanted to go somewhere far, and possibly to have an overnight trip. I desired no less—after all, the JRS covered our costs. We settled for Liwonde National Park, a reserve with numerous mammals, reptiles, and birds, shared by three distinct districts—Machinga, Mangochi, and Liwonde—in the southern part of Malawi. This trip would take more than ten hours of bus travel each way, partly because of the roads, but also partly because we were a bunch of dunderheads—whatever that means—who constantly disturbed the driver. It was exciting!

My father accompanied me to school on the day we departed. He was more excited than I was. What else could a parent desire other than to see his child have a free day to explore just for pleasure, unconstrained by the refugee's chains! I had a little backpack in which we placed a few *mandazi,* or fat cakes, and a significant amount of squash juice to drink along the way. My mother had fried some *karanga* for me to eat while I traveled. When we arrived at school, our eyes were met by the stares of other equally excited children, all waiting eagerly for two buses that the JRS had rented from the city. One for the boys, one for the girls.

In addition to the more than eighty young people from the refugee camp, there were a couple of staff members; some were members of the club, some were not. We left school around eleven in the morning, just when the sun was smiling its best. It was a long, fascinating journey: from Dowa through Lilongwe, where I admired the greenery of the capital city and also the new parliament building at Capitol Hill that was being inaugurated, to Baraka where the roads to Zomba and Blantyre diverged, and finally to the Liwonde town center where we briefly stopped and I bought roasted fish directly caught from the Shire River—the longest river in Malawi. It was all enjoyable and a little too noisy! You can imagine the zeal of excited young teens who rarely got the chance to move beyond the camp premises past the area of Chief Msakambewa, whose territory hosted the refugee camp. While in Liwonde, I was buying some snacks from a vendor and paying from the bus window when a pickpocket pulled at my arm trying to snatch the twenty kwacha from my fingers, the only money I had received from my loving parents. Fortunately, I overpowered him, but my arm was bruised from the pulling and the friction against the window frame.

When we left the Liwonde town center with less than two kilometers remaining before we entered the national park, the battery of our bus failed. It made an explosive sound that sent all of us into terrified screams—more flashback than mere ordinary fear! For the next couple of hours, we had to wait for the replacement battery to be brought to us in the middle of nowhere, in the stillness of the night.

We finally made it to the park and arrived at the Chinguni Lodge's reception a few minutes past midnight. The receptionist welcomed us and lectured us with endless instructions on how we were to behave. He was a very cool middle-aged man with a strong Malawian accent. I was particularly critical about that, as I somehow sensed what was to follow.

I was asked to deliver a thankful speech, a speech in which I made a joke of myself. It had been a few months since I first started learning English. With my friends at school, we normally communicated with three of the languages spoken in the camp—Swahili, Kinyarwanda (closely related to Kirundi), and sometimes French. There were more languages, of course, like Arabic and Amharic for those from the Horn of Africa, and Lingala and Kibembe from the DRC, but I did not speak those. I rarely spoke English outside of school, but here I was having to deliver a speech in English. I tried, confidently, but with little ease. I had a strong French accent and in my attempts to indicate how we were "more than happy" to be there, I pronounced "more" as "*mowa,*" which happened to be one of the local traditional beers in Dowa district along with *kachasu* and *mugorigori*. My clubmates burst into laughter which followed me during the entire trip as I naturally became "Mr. Mowa."

The next day, we woke up early in the morning to have breakfast. We were visited by numerous monkeys and baboons that waited eagerly to eat the remainders of our white bread and margarine. Some of us had the guts to share with the animals, even though it was prohibited. I was fascinated seeing these humanlike creatures for the first time and to observe the way they looked at us, the way they grabbed the food we gave them and stuffed it in their mouths. It was charming!

We then had a tour of the park as we headed to Mvuu Camp, which was carefully perched on the bank of the Shire River. The beautiful view of the river itself, the hippopotamus that faded into the water and reappeared a few minutes later to gasp a huge volume of air, and the crocodiles that floated, carefree, were all quite mesmerizing. Later, a tour guide cheerfully narrated the history of the park and described some conservation projects that were taking place. I was enthralled to learn that Liwonde was the only park in Southern Africa to have Lilian's lovebirds, a rare species of brightly colored birds, and that the park management went as far as Kruger National Park in South Africa to ship in lions for the sake of conservation.

On our way back, we encountered two massive elephants. The girls' bus was ahead of ours, and upon seeing the elephants the girls screamed so much that the driver had to accelerate past them in haste! The boys, however, asked our driver to drive much slower and to stop if possible. We watched the two elephants saunter majestically toward us. They were so big—much bigger than any other animal I had ever seen. We had been warned not to climb out of the window but instead observe any unfolding scene from our seats, as silently as we could. This was hard to keep to, but the excitement mixed with a small amount of fear forced us to behave. I wished I had a camera to capture that moment and those that would follow!

Every experience felt real and lifelike. I felt so much joy for the first time in a very long while and I couldn't help but think of the days when I used to run in the hills and valleys, hunting birds from below the massive canopies back home. How I wanted to go back to my childhood!

Sooner than we wished, we had to go back to our prison. We passed through Salima, a district in the central region of Malawi, known mainly for its beautiful beaches along Lake Malawi. This was a different route from the one we had taken on our way to Liwonde. Somewhere on the way back was a big burning bus encircled by many drivers who had cautiously parked their cars at a distance, along with other spectators who were watching it burn to ashes. The passengers were all standing miserably in the light created by the flames, watching in horror like everyone else. As we passed by the scene I closed my eyes tightly, because the sight brought back the traumatic experiences I have had with fires. It felt horrible! The next day this incident was all over the news. No one had been hurt, but everyone's belongings had been lost.

We arrived back in the refugee camp around three in the morning. Returning felt awkward and sad; I wished I could have stayed in Liwonde National Park. I wanted to live like those monkeys, free spirits in every way, or like those hippos, crocodiles, and birds, having the time of my life in water and air without anyone suppressing my free will, or like those elephants, which were scary to some but so admirable in many ways. I wanted to go back and be all alone there, to just be all by myself.

Unfortunately, wishes are just wishes! Over the coming days I experienced a strong nostalgia that faded softly and slowly, overcome by the will to survive. And the zeal to thrive.

We sat in our tiny grocery shop, just my father and me. My mother might have been inside the house struggling with her normal frailties or just hiding from the ever-accumulating dust. In early July, the camp gets dry and very windy. To make matters worse, our grocery shop—"Inthemba," we called it—directly faced a cross-junctional walkway. The path that stretched from the entrance of our shop led to an open area of about twenty square meters. Straight ahead from our shop along this track was a mosque, and on its left a library, one of my favorite spots in the camp. There was a borehole between the two, and the whole space was surrounded by grass-thatched residences. These grass-thatched roofs on top of mud-bricked structures were the most touristy attractions the camp had to offer. We lived and ate in them, especially when it was too windy to be outside. This open area contributed to the despicable dust that accumulated in our shop and on our groceries. I hated every single hour spent with the dust, which was often every single hour of the day. This broad path, along which we had rented our house, was commonly used as a marketplace. The commodities ranged from shoes and secondhand clothes to sugarcane and different types of vegetables. I always delighted in looking at the ladies, refugees and Malawians alike, who sold *rape*, *chinese,* and *kabitchi*—the most popular vegetables.

From time to time, I would discreetly help myself to either a biscuit or some *mandasi* from the shop to satisfy my cravings. I think my father knew. I did it all the time when he was not around, and sometimes even when he was around but too busy to notice. I always looked forward to those moments whenever we were in the school holidays. I had completed Grade 8, the last year of primary school, and the holidays were a bit too long. Here I sat, eating and talking to my father as I reminisced on the recent past.

On the last day of school, when we collected our school reports and marked the end of each school term, I was seized by unusually high spirits—unusual, because happiness is the least likely state of mind one can expect as a refugee. I was happy because I knew presents were always awaiting me: presents from the JRS, the school, and my impoverished family (my mother and father, to be specific). I worked my fingers to the bone, spending many sleepless hours reading and revising notes in our dimly lit decrepit houses, turning pages of various books in the camp library to supplement all that I did not understand in class, and often pestering my teachers and my father to satisfy my endless curiosity in the sciences, or to mark the unassigned assignments I did independently. I assumed control over my time whenever I was not in church or slaving for the family, and in turn, the first position in class was reserved for me. Chichewa was the only subject that I flunked, but sometimes I sat with friends during the exam to get the mark I desired. It felt unusual, very unlike me, but I kept in mind that a man must survive even when it calls for negative deeds. Although I found the fearsome English language easy, learning it cost me the gradual loss of my cherished childhood language, French, as I redirected all my mental energy toward learning English.

The presents I received at the end of every term were appealing and motivational. Soccer balls, shoes, pants, and other items from the JRS; notebooks and pens from the school; and ten or twenty kwacha from my parents. These were the benefits of being the best in class. I had to start involving myself in family issues such as helping my father in the shop. In the early days when we did not have the shop, I did other things too, such as selling *karanga*—fried groundnuts.

Throughout the holidays, I had to walk in circles around the whole refugee camp carrying nicely packed *karanga*. Usually, my older brother bought the dried groundnuts from the nearby villages using a borrowed bike. Sometimes I accompanied him. We would argue about whether we should say "Tikufuna *msawa*" or "Tikufuna *msawawa*"—"We want groundnuts" or "We want peas" in Chichewa—and to this day I still do not know which means what! Sometimes, we went as far as twenty kilometers away from the camp periphery, encroaching into the sparsely populated *Midzi* (the Chewa villages).

Our greatest worry was always the possibility of encountering the Zilombo—the Chewa traditional dancers of Gule Wamkulu, figures believed to have come from the graveyards. Often masked and fully disguised in all sorts of weird costumes, the Zilombo did not speak human languages. They produced only weird sounds and walked with weapons. It is best not to cross their path, especially if you are a foreigner and they happen to discern that! Depending on their mood, they could beat you severely to the point of death. But they could also be friendly if you had something to offer them—normally money, especially in the form of coins. I always wondered what sort of legendary figures they were if they craved the worldly riches that should obviously be of no use to them. But did I believe in such things as "ghosts" and "magic" and "beings that rose from their graves" in the first place? Regardless, we met them a few times and often immediately changed our direction.

Entering these obscure villages looking for *msawa* or *msawawa*, whichever it was, as well as taking some casual promenades with my father, was also another way of exploring Malawian culture. Apart from meeting the Zilombo, I was always excited to see how men were greeted by women. When a lady, young or old, met an older man in the way, she would have to step off the road, kneel or squat, and say "Zikomo zikomo" repeatedly while periodically clapping her hands until the man walked past her. The word *Zikomo* means "thank you," but here it was used as a gesture of respect. I had never seen this before but I loved to see it, notably because it reminded me of the culture of mine that I no longer possessed. When my brother and I arrived in the homesteads of the Malawians, we also imitated their respectful calls by calling loudly "Odi odi kuno" ("Hello, there") or "Zikomo zikomo," depending on which first came to our minds.

We were often unsuccessful in getting groundnuts, but when we did we cracked open the shells to remove the needed peanuts, working as a family. We selected the best, and either my mother or one of my two elder sisters would fry them. We packed them in twenty-milliliter plastic bags that I had to carry around the camp. This was my main responsibility, partly because everyone else felt too old to do it.

"Karanga, karanga, karanga—imekarangiwa bobo!" I would holler in Swahili, adding and emphasizing the Chichewa slang "bobo," a word adapted from the French "bon." "Fried groundnuts, fried groundnuts, fried groundnuts—they are well fried!" I would holler at the top of my fragile voice to attract attention. "Ten kwacha, ten kwacha, ten kwacha ..." was another repeating call I used, especially when I was close to other miserable boys or girls like me fighting for their families' survival.

There were also school holidays where my elder brother and I had to start making bricks to sell. Many more refugees were flocking to the camp, and so more mud-and-brick, grass-thatched houses were needed to accommodate them. We would compete with many other young people to make the best bricks and sell them at a cheaper price. We managed to raise a small amount of money for the family and for ourselves. I often bought *mandazi* or *sambusa*, two types of homemade cakes, after cracking some hard arithmetic to make sure that there was enough profit so that my father wouldn't notice.

In the early days of living in the camp, we were able to buy salt, soap, and sugar for my mother's life-saving *chai* (tea) through these two economic activities. With this, we established the first *inthemba* right within our living compound in Blantyre—with my father's hustling and external assistance, naturally, although I would like to give myself considerable credit for this. After all, I often experienced dehydration due to walking mornings, middays, and afternoons under the unforgiving, scorching sun selling the stuff. I endured intimidation and dismissal just to get this basic skill that helped transform my family's ugly situation.

We did not sell much in our first grocery shop: just *karanga*, *mawesa* (palm oil), soap, and other cheap household essentials. The business went well, and soon my father upgraded to the new *inthemba*, for which he paid minimal rent. This location was where we were based and where I would spend my school breaks.

Through friends and other connections, my father managed to lease a small farm as well. It was located about a hundred meters beyond the primary school. The camp management had secured some farms around the inhabited areas, where the land had initially been meant to accommodate more refugees. Since this part of the camp was bare, some refugees had claimed different sections of it and were able to cultivate different types of crops ranging from legumes, like beans and soya, to vegetables such as cabbages and tomatoes, to starchy roots like cassava. There were some who went a step farther and planted banana plantains—a crop native to the African tropics that would not grow in the south or north of the continent under normal climatic conditions.

We were extremely happy to have a piece of land where we could spend our energy and hope for life.

By this time, we had already planted and harvested some maize, and this had marked a milestone in our family. Farming brought us together because it involved almost the whole household. Even when my mother was too weak to seize the hoe or the *panga* knife, she would cook porridge using the minimal mealy flour available in the house, or she would prepare some tea with powdered milk. The farming season typically started in late October or early November, since the first rains usually began in late November or early December. After clearing the land, tilling and planting the corns, weeding, and performing all sorts of intermediate steps and activities, we would relax a little and visit the field from time to time for other minor activities such as applying fertilizer. I always marveled at how the maize crops grew, and with Mr. Phiri as my agriculture teacher, I often visited to monitor the crops to see if they had germinated and if they were indeed as green as green could be. Let's just say that I was a little curious.

One thing I never enjoyed throughout the farming season was the *waganyu*, the local Malawians who came to beg for work from the wealthy refugees (or refugees who pretended to be wealthy) in exchange for food or other commodities. It was a common practice, and my father hired them when he needed an extra hand because he never wanted to discourage us or keep us occupied instead of letting us fully concentrate on our studies while in school—the most crucial aspect in life, according to him. But it pained me to see the local people, who have received and to some extent even assimilated foreigners, being the ones begging for work. How ironic! Certainly, Malawi is a poor country. A significant majority of the population lives under the poverty line. Yet I never understood why this ought to be the case. Even worse, seeing these people, often men and women in their mid-thirties, forties, or even older carrying hoes and calling out "Zikomo Zikomo" to capture the attention of those who would pity them, brought me some negative feelings about life and the struggles we go through every day to survive. I looked at the people and thought to myself, "This could be my mother," or "Maybe she is a widow." I looked at the men and concocted stories of how they did not have farms and could not send their kids to school, which would only trap their next generation within the poverty cycle. Sometimes *waganyu* came in the form of young people loitering around, and these were often preferred for their energy. I sympathized with them and noticed how privileged I was to be in a school constructed by the JRS, even if my life on its own was never assured the possibility of having a tomorrow.

However, I also often wondered who I was to have such thoughts! After all, being a refugee, I was just a wanderer, lost in a large pool of uncertainties where searching for opportunities was a gamble that made those who put their hearts and souls into the game heartless and unfeeling. I was just a helpless character in a play whose stage was filled with misery and quests for survival—constant struggles to see the sun the next day. Being young in the refugee camp, I was a vulnerable being exposed to all sorts of misfortunes like turning into a crooked pickpocket such as the friends I saw to becoming a drug and sex addicts, with no thoughts about the future whatsoever. These thoughts scared me, and I never stopped thinking about them—whether in school, selling groundnuts, making bricks, or even while I farmed with my family. Seeing the *waganyu* was also another mind-boggling experience that spoke to me, telling me that it was not only in the refugee camps where children died of marasmus and kwashiorkor, where old women were buried due to degenerative diseases caused by lack of proper food and sanitation, where men simply went crazy, committed murder, and were jailed. It was a reminder that forsaken, poverty-stricken communities are everywhere and that they can be any group of people, not just those of us who had left our beloved motherland to seek comfort and safety. More importantly, it was a reminder of who I did not want to be, of where I did not want my family to end up. This inspired me to work hard in school, help my family get some money, and to simply survive.

I hoped that my hard work would pay off. The *inthemba* was already one result, even if I played a minor role in getting it built. I could always muse inside with my father.

Whenever I was alone with my father, as was the case this day, we often had father-to-son talks. We talked about religion, the mess in our country, Africa, and the world; we spoke of education, family issues, and so on. Now that I had completed Grade 8, hoping to get the best results and to go to a good high school (I only had one in mind), my father would listen with much keenness as

I told him some of my dreams, like how I wanted to be a musician, a medical doctor, a writer—everything! He had a particular interest in my strong desire to impact societies positively and on a large scale. He knew, from years of observation and chitchat, that one important option I had in mind was becoming a Catholic priest. In fact, I wonder if he had ever considered the possibility of that not becoming an option, too. He and my mother, and almost any family friend we had encountered, were convinced of my future priesthood beyond any doubt. They were certain that I would make a good priest, and I had convinced myself of it too. This conviction defined my behavior, the kind of schools I envisioned for myself, and how I approached what was required for me to get to where I wanted to be.

But conviction is what makes up faith and faith is what comprises religion. And religion has a lot of issues!

My father and I talked about anything, really, and he never judged. He is a wonderful father, one among a countable few.

We were listening to Radio Alinafe, a private Catholic radio station based at Maula Cathedral in Lilongwe, when, miraculously, they started announcing the names of those admitted into the three most prestigious missionary schools countrywide: Likuni Boys Secondary School, Likuni Girls Secondary School, and Ludzi Girls Secondary school. All three were Catholic missionary schools. I was so keen to hear my name!

I had taken the entrance examinations the previous month, in June. We started at the parish level. The camp's Catholic community identified itself with Nanthomba parish, the only parish in the Dowa district. That was where we had the first selection exams, in which I had excelled and placed among the top three students. I was praised by both the priest and the church leaders in the camp, as well as by my parents, who were extremely excited for me. I had convinced my father that Likuni Boys Secondary School (LIBOSS) was the place for me ever since I had heard of it. To me, it seemed like the best school in the whole country. Even more, a Rwandan refugee orphan who attended Likuni Girls Secondary School had topped the whole country in the Form 4 national exams, and the Malawian government had swiftly offered her citizenship and a scholarship for studying in China. I was hopeful! After I passed my parish-level test, it was time to compete at the provincial level, and for this we went to Salima district.

I really enjoyed the tests we were given! Religious knowledge was my forte—after all, I was very active in church and had a strong Catholic background. Mathematics was among my strengths too. When it came to science, anything was possible for learners under a teacher called Mr. Mazibuko, or "Mazibuko-mana," as he usually called himself. He was funny and made science seem so practical and pleasurable. "Mazibuko-mana" was his attempt to sound as if he had a refugee name because most Rwandan and Burundian names ended with "mana," which literally means "God." Unfortunately, Mr. Mazibuko died of lung cancer few years after I left Malawi, as he was a heavy smoker. I will never forget how fascinating he made every lesson through pairing everything he taught with a sexual joke.

After the examination, I excitedly exited the testing room with a relaxed face, bragging about how easy the exams were, although Nifasha, a friend who went together with me in a group of three refugees from the parish, did not share the same enthusiasm.

Now, almost a month later, it was time to prove to my father that all my conviction about studying in LIBOSS was in fact a prophecy. He had never believed I could get into LIBOSS, mainly because of our status and circumstances at the time. Thanks to his peers, who convinced him that the best thing to do was to encourage me, he succumbed to their pressure and promised to pay for anything I needed if I made it. He was determined to send me to LIBOSS even if it called for him to sell our *inthemba*!

By luck or by God's will, we were both listening to Radio Alinafe when it happened—which we rarely did. Only my elder brother listened to Malawian radio stations such as Radio Alinafe, searching for cool music mostly to calm his temper and deal with agitation of camp life. I loved his taste in music!

There was a pause in whatever we were doing. Thank God, there were no customers to disturb the loud silence that had quickly seized the two of us. Most people in the camp were penniless, and we sometimes spent minutes to hours without even a single person asking for the price of cooking oil. The awkward moment lasted much longer than we had expected, as our growing curiosity got the better of us. An experienced thief could have easily taken plenty from our counter as we listened to the radio reporters who read out the names of the successful candidates one by one.

First, the reporters announced the list of those who would soon be in Likuni Girls Secondary School. I listened with interest but with little concern—I just wanted

47

to know if a classmate from the camp or any other girl from the parish with whom we had gone to Salima were one of them. There was none. Then followed Likuni Boys Secondary School, which captured all of my attention, as well as my father's. My classmate, Nifasha Elias, was among the first twenty students called. "Nifasha Elias wochokera ku Nathomba Parish, Dowa," so the reporter said. I felt a leap of faith in me: if Nifasha had made it, why not me? I felt a bit more relaxed by that, but as they called out more names, my body and mind grew tense. When they finished the list, my name was not there!

I have had a few injections in hospital. Once, I was given five successive injections in less than ten minutes by a practicing nurse who really did not know what she was doing. I was a kid by then, maybe six or seven years old. My sister had cried while she watched in fear and confusion. I had been a very strong man for not shedding a single tear, as if the injections were not happening to my body. This time, however, as I realized that my name was not on the list, this familiar situation came back with an unimaginable magnitude. I first felt my body itching. Then when my father looked at me with his sad, consoling face, I felt like a million injections were being pushed into and pulled out of my fragile, youthful body. I felt like a million bees had stung me at once and like my mind had started its own rotation against that of the earth itself.

Voluminous tears condensed in my eyes, but I refused to give up hope. I knew there must have been a mistake. After all, I had had too much faith in God and in myself. I had worked hard!

I wished Alberto were there, to at least have someone to share the bitter feeling of sadness and despair with. The bitter feeling of failure. He was the sole person I could think of who could ease the tense atmosphere and make my nerves feel a little less perturbed. Maybe he would have said, "My brother, it is God's will. We will still make it far." Or swaggered, "The stupid news anchor forgot the most important name of them all. … He should be ashamed of himself." Or perhaps he would have looked at me in utter sympathetic silence as well, because he knew more than anybody else how much I wanted to be at LIBOSS. Either way, he was absent. My own self was absent from the scene too. How was it possible?

The reporter continued, and I felt it would be worth it to at least listen more, just to know if my female classmate had been accepted, to Ludzi Girls Secondary School. My father listened with me, just for support.

Her name was not called.

On the contrary, towards the end, I heard something like "Gene-Mitshelle Koffy-I," probably a reporter struggling to pronounce my (then) French name, "Jean Michel Koffi." Immediately, my melancholy was followed by maximal confusion.

"A girls' school?" I wondered aloud.

CHAPTER 2:

DIM LIGHT

I marveled at the way my father and I trod triumphantly on the tar road that branched from where the minibus had dropped us. I had not heard much of this place, and everything looked quite different from anything I had ever imagined.

When we took a minibus from the bus station in Lilongwe that very same morning, I had thought we were heading to another part of the inner city. Lilongwe was beautiful from my perspective. I was particularly enchanted by the greenness I saw all around. But I hated one thing most: the tumult and clamorous noise. Loudspeakers were everywhere, and all of them played different Malawian songs from the new hip-hop mix by Mafunyeta, who was quickly gaining popularity, to other interesting and quite renowned Malawian singers like Skeffa Chimoto and Lucius Banda, to Malawian gospel choirs like the Zomba Cathedral, Kasungu CCAP (Church of Central African Presbyterian), and so on. I heard no foreign songs. I kept wondering how physics explained that nuisance in terms of sound waves, frequencies, and constructive and destructive interferences. I had read about these things in a science book at the camp library.

The area was dirty too, completely contradicting my idealized perspective of a city—especially a capital city. It seemed to me the municipality did not try to control waste disposals, and people were happy with their surroundings being that way. Vendors were everywhere selling all sorts of things. Their high-pitched voices attempted to attract customers and exacerbated the clamorous atmosphere, and they set me to thinking about the days when I sold *karanga*. I realized that now that I was going to a boarding school, I would probably never do that again. This thought made me smile, and my father glanced at me but remained silent. Every minute the vendors sold; the more they sold, the dirtier the place got. Buyers dropped plastic bags and industrial packages indiscriminately. For some reason, my thoughts took me back to Mr. Bondondo and our social science classes. *Laxity on the city council's part.* I smiled again.

Everywhere around me people were eating mice, nicely arranged on small sticks. That captivated me for a long while. I couldn't imagine myself eating mice! As I stared at these mice eaters, I started thinking about some talks I had had with Alberto and a few other friends about how foreigners conceived of our cultures' mythical views.

"Sikia mwanangu, kwani umekula nyoka leo?" Alberto would cynically ask me if I had eaten a snake that day.

"No … Today we've had frogs in our pots." I would respond, giggling. "They took so long to cook that we decided to throw them away, thinking they were growing tails." The frogs growing tails was my favorite quip.

"By the way, we beheaded our chicken yesterday. It's been moving around since then. Magic!" One of us would interject lightheartedly.

At this point we would both burst into uncontrolled laughter, cherishing each other's opinionated approach to life, cultures, and traditions. We criticized the ignorance held by people who did not know about where we came from. Later in life, I would learn about stereotypes and generalizations, and about how Africa's image is highly colored by ignorance and the media. I was afraid that at school I was going to miss all these wonderful friends and the beautiful conversations that we had. Especially Alberto. He had been my other half ever since we met.

Born on the same day in the same month and year, we considered ourselves twins. Having had time to listen to his inner thoughts, his mistreatment by his family, his dependence on his friends, and so on, I thought he would be missing a part of himself as well when I left. Now that I was leaving him behind to attend a boarding school, it dawned on me how worthy he was. We spent most of our time together: at school during break time, at church singing, in the street that ran right below our houses playing *kalele*—the rural version of football named and played by some young boys, and fetching water at the boreholes. Our friendship rose above brotherhood; it was indescribable. I couldn't imagine the whole school term, three whole months, without him. Little did I know that the future had decided differently! For the next stretch of time—I do not know for how long—he occupied my mind as the minibus cruised on. We were out of the inner city sooner than I had expected.

The areas outside the inner city, however, seemed more serene and organized. The minibus continued to crawl, kilometer after kilometer, away from the main city. Before I knew it, I had lost my sense of direction. I couldn't tell East from West. Shortly, my father was told that we had arrived and that we had to walk a short distance of two hundred meters to reach our destination.

As we kept on the tar road, trees on both sides of it, I observed an enormous structure blurred by the tree branches. I soon discovered it was a church. A very old church, built in a traditional rectangular way. It was Likuni Parish. Then I knew we had reached, that we had finally arrived at LIBOSS. My father looked at my excitement and, through the corner of my eyes, I could see that his wonderful smile was slowly growing. He had probably waited for this day for a long time. Of course, my admission to LIBOSS posed a financial burden to him, but he was a man. He has always been. I am sure he was happy to see me leaving the refugee camp for a while. Besides, he had one fewer teenager to take care of. My thoughts would soon be confirmed when I was told that he had established one more *inthemba* in Sangano, a remote area in the southern part of Malawi, a few weeks after I started school. (Sangano is located between Malawi and Mozambique. The street that separates both countries was ideal for refugees. Whenever the refugees detected immigration officers threatening to ask for documentation, they simply closed their shops and walked to the other side of the road. They would then gladly watch the show as the officers scratched their heads, because by diplomatic law the officers could not pursue a person who is in a different country.)

We continued down the road and finally arrived at a gate with an inscription that said, "Ora et Labora." My father immediately translated it for me, being the genius that he is: "It means 'Work and Pray,'" he mumbled in our native language.

There were other students, many of whose suitcases were being searched. I wondered what the security officers were looking for. Some seemed to be there for a reunion, while others' faces displayed a considerable amount of distraction or confusion. I encountered the gigantic hall in the school, the open area where the grass was carefully tended, separated into sections by walking paths with bricks on either side, and the apparently old blocks—the classes—that made an open rectangle in their midst. I looked at all the different individuals and imagined who among them would become my first friend. I felt a bit scared and insecure. A refugee still struggling with Chichewa, speaking an English characterized by a strong French accent from my childhood, I wondered if I would be accepted by my soon-to-be schoolmates. The thought of having friends, too … Well, I first had to ascertain that the school administration had confirmed my place here.

After hearing from Radio Alinafe that I had been sent to a girls' school, I had instantly taken my father's bike, which I often had no permission to ride, and rushed to my former primary school, Umodzi Katubza Full Primary School. There was a teacher there who was a very active member of our Catholic community in the camp. He had guided me and my friends through the process of taking the entrance examination and was also very close to the parish priest. He had also persuaded my father to motivate me to apply by convincing me, or rather assuring me, that my school fees would be provided for if I passed.

After explaining the matter to him, he had immediately phoned Father Chembe, a now-deceased parish priest, who immediately rang up the cathedral, who immediately called up Likuni Boys Secondary School, who immediately called someone else. When I heard of the process, it seemed to me a long and complicated chain, but fascinating regardless. Fame! I was known before I even stepped in the school, and that seemed to work positively in the direction of my dreams!

As soon as we talked to the secretary, she told us to be patient and wait for a while as Brother Murakho, the head administrator at the time, was busy. But within a few minutes, he appeared with his remarkable protruding belly, apparent elegance, and his demeanor of both intelligence and wisdom. On seeing the two of us, he gave us a friendly smile.

As he stretched out his hand to meet my father's, he said words that stimulated both my mind and body: "So, you are 'Jean Michel' who was mistakenly placed in Ludzi Girls Secondary School?" He pronounced *Jean Michel* with a particular French emphasis.

I did not know whether it was a question or just a state-ment. Maybe more of a rhetorical question. I was a little bit flattered. He proceeded, and his next words changed an aspect of me, most probably for my entire life.

"They thought, eh hmm …" he paused for a while, keenly looking at me, "… that your name was a girl's name, because *Jean* is not very common here in Malawi, and in many English-speaking countries too."

Who thought what? Did I not indicate that I was male during the examinations? What does a name have to do with English-speaking countries anyway? My mind did its best to question every aspect of these words, but my mouth betrayed me by refusing to utter a single word. Maybe this was a mere excuse! If it were in the present, I would have thought about how names relate to gender identity and whether that changes depending on whose former colony you were in. Thousands of thoughts ran through my mind like charged electrons in a circuit. It was an epiphany.

And from then on, I was no longer myself. I became John Michael Koffi. *Inwardly.*

The third term began on the sixteenth of April. I had returned to the now-familiar place. James Chandamale, my school "father," had been very helpful and friendly. A "father" was a student in his final year whom the school selected to guide newcomers—a friend assigned by the school to look after you while you were lost and confused. I was lucky that he was a responsible house prefect. He lived in Rukuru House and my life there was magnificent! He never exploited me, like most other "fathers" did to their "sons." This new term was his last at the school, together with the rest of his classmates. Little did I know, it was my last too.

Thinking about him usually made me think of the first day when Brother Murakho had directed him to me. James had been expecting me and was excited to have me. Had he heard anything about me? Had he known the scandalous mismatch of my name and my gender that had redirected me to a girl's school and not my most desired LIBOSS? I never asked.

In his quest to help me adapt as quickly and simply as possible, James ran helter-skelter around the school premises with me on my very first day, looking for a bed frame inscribed "220," which was my school number. It was my personal identification number, which I was supposed to keep for the next four years of my LIBOSS journey. *Any* school property under my custody had to have the number engraved on it, including my bed, books, and furniture. He explained all this in our very first delightful interaction. He also joked, although his sense of humor was not terribly acute.

"You look like your father!" James had said, as we ran up and down the beautifully trimmed green pastures of LIBOSS. One thing I love about missionary schools is their sense of beauty and order. Likuni boys was run by Marist Brothers, and the appearance of the different corners of the school truly reflected the quality of education they offered. Beautiful gardens, stunning flowers all around, especially near the residence situated directly on the left of the main entrance into the school compound, opposite the back wing of the famous and colossal Likuni Boys Hall.

"Yes," I replied shyly. Not that I thought it was true, but I did not know what else to say.

"So, where do you originally come from?"

"I am from the DRC."

"You live in the refugee camp?"

"Hmm ... well ... yes!" I struggled to process the question, to answer him. I was so afraid to be called a *Muburundi*, as the Malawians referred to any refugee. The thought of different students within the school premises and elsewhere pointing at me, muttering "Tamuone Muburundi uyo" (look at this *Muburundi*), scared me! The first people to flee to Malawi were Burundians. The local people called them "Maburundi," a new word to add to the endless Chichewa vocabulary, and naturally every subsequent generation of refugees, whether Congolese, Rwandan, Ethiopian, Somalian or other, inherited the beautifully repulsive moniker. Stigmatization, belittlement, and discrimination were some *charakararistics* of the Maburundi experience. And I dreaded that!

"Don't worry, son," James quickly noted, realizing my fear of being recognized for who I was. "You can tell me anything. I won't tell anyone what you wouldn't tell them yourself." A lot of "telling" in his words, I feared! But his calm nature and spirit convinced me of his good caliber, and I felt at ease with him.

We eventually found the bed and had to wait for the mattress. My beloved sister had sweated so that I could get some presentable bedsheets to ensure that I would fit into my new community!

Later that day I sat in his room in the corner next to the main entrance of the hostel square. The room was shared by all the prefects in Rukuru, regardless of what their duties were. We had four hostels all together, and arranged to form a closed square. I always marveled at how that arrangement gave me a sense of security. I knew the place was closed off, and whenever we were in the two small entrances could be locked, preventing any unwanted visitors. Such was my history with break-ins and violence!

He asked me some basic questions as we chatted, and his calmness seemed to stand out over that of the other prefects. Nonetheless he remained relatively careful with me, and although he had helped me in everything, he still seemed slightly reserved. I hoped it had nothing to do with my being a foreigner. I also learned that one of his friends was a guy from the refugee camp, which explained how he had probably already known me before I arrived.

We were five students from Dzaleka, yet none of us a refugee. The refugee identity was not one we wanted to have. Perhaps we did not want to be reminded of who we were: the *Maburundi*. Only the administration knew, and those closest to us.

In public, I was a Zambian—from the town of Livingstone in the far South of the country—to make it more convincing. I had attended an international school that was taught in French, so I did not speak English properly. My friend, Nifasha Elias, and two others—one in Form 2 and the other in Form 3, were Tanzanians. They had come all the way from neighboring Tanzania to study in Malawi. One of us, who happened to be James's friend and classmate, was a Malawian. These were some of the skeletons we guarded in our cupboards. Very fragile.

I was used to the school and to missing Alberto by my third term. I seldom visited the camp since I started school at LIBOSS because I lived with my father during the holidays and helped him in the shop. I missed my church and friends back in the camp. Funny enough, I missed riding bikes with my brother and going *kumidzi* to look for *msawawa*, and tilling the soil with maximum energy hoping to see the *chimanga* (maize crops) grow. But none of these memories troubled me, as there were many more pressing issues.

Dr. Bingu wa Mutharikha, the former president of Malawi, passed away on Good Friday of that year. Suddenly, there was political instability throughout the whole country. Refugees' shops and wholesalers had been targeted, some even robbed. My father's shop in Sangano had been robbed, too, as it was being set up. Thankfully, his refugee friends from other towns and cities kindly put up precious pennies to help him reestablish the shop! Every single refugee with a family to take care of was worried about how the conditions might turn out. Cars were being set on fire in Blantyre, as reported by Zodiac, one of the major radio stations in Malawi. The situation worsened each day. We were all afraid for the future of Malawi. All this time, the news set me thinking about what I missed from back home.

Simultaneous to the aggravating social and political instability were more personal issues. My mother had been struggling with heart problems for quite a while, and she got even worse now that the solace, peace, and tranquility she had hoped to see in Malawi was fading away. My sister's daughter had undefined allergies. We had initially assumed it was our cat, Katze, but after Katze sadly passed on it was clear that we had unjustly accused it! Perhaps it was the environment itself. The refugee camp has its own ways of killing slowly. People always wondered the nationality of the next person to be put to rest. The most recent case was a Rwandan family friend of ours who slept one day and did not wake up the next, when she seemed in good shape otherwise. It had been puzzling and scary to me, and probably to my siblings, because the lady was around the same age as my mother, and they both had similar health problems. Had I not had the chance to move in with my father in Sangano, I would definitely have had many other contributing factors to my subconscious distress. These realities stayed much longer, but they would soon all temporarily fade from my psyche.

Less than three weeks after our return, we experienced one of the most fascinating LIBOSS traditions. In both the second and third term of school, the best students in each class were awarded money as a way to recognize their endeavors. The school awarded different sums of money to the best three students by subject, class level, and department. I had received a considerable amount from them as the first student the previous term, having excelled in both the language and science departments with the highest score in several subjects. This day, however, was slightly different.

It was my day. No one in the history of LIBOSS—except for the renowned Joe Lilema, a finalist during my first year who happened to be Zambian—had ever managed to set the standards I set. The students' eyes were wide open as I got called to the stage over and over again. They clapped for the first five times I went up, and then they gave up. I was confused too, because every time I turned my back to head into the crowd of students, my name would be called again. In the end, I decided to stand still facing the deputy head teacher calling the names from the stage, and waited until all the calling was done.

I had not expected that to happen. I was extremely happy and puzzled. According to my school report, I knew I stood taller academically than any of the ninety other first years. I had no question that I was the best in all the departments and that I had the highest marks in seven of the nine subjects. It was only in Chichewa and Agriculture where I had not attained the highest marks in my grade, and I was not surprised because these two were my least favorite. In any case, I was astounded by this turn of events.

As I stood on the stage in utmost confusion, my exhilaration mixed with fear; I wondered who to look at. LIBOSS had one of the biggest and best entertainment halls in Lilongwe. This was also where we conducted our assemblies, and where the whole student body wrote their end-of-term exams and national exams. The main stage was raised approximately one-and-a-half meters from the audience platform. I stood in my black shoes and marveled! Our school uniform comprised grey socks, dark blue long trousers, and a sky-blue shirt with the school's logo. The shirt was beautifully tightened on top with a necktie, and often covered by a dark blue jersey. The necktie was made of dark blue segments separated by light or sky-blue oblique patterns. The school jersey also had two sky-blue stripes at the terminus of each long sleeve, and at both the bottom and top ends; "LBSS" was engraved in sky-blue letters on the left part of the chest. I often admired how beautiful we all looked in the school uniform, blue being my favorite color, and as I stood among the teachers and students, feeling delighted and shy, I imagined how different we all were no matter how similar they wanted us to be.

I had proved to be different. In my religious life, obedient nature, hard work, commitment to sports and duties, and analytical approach to life at LIBOSS, I was simply different. And now another aspect entered the equation: a sum of money equaling almost half my school fees for that term. Was I the boy with the most prizes or rather the most-prized boy? All I knew was that it was a great day, one against all odds!

I had gained both reputation and respect, as well as a strong feeling of achievement.

"You are entering Form 2 next September," my history teacher, Mr. Chikazinga, observed. He looked at me intently, a serious look that I found odd given his usual cheerful self and his wise yet simple approach to life.

"Yes, sir," I answered, quite ignorant of what the future had in store for me.

"You are not only competing with your classmates here, but with more than a hundred thousand others from across the country." His tone was dense and sincere. This conversation took place after I had passed his test with excellent marks while the rest of the class had flunked helplessly. He had taught us the history of Africa and about civilizations and kingdoms—a subject that, weirdly enough, had deeply caught my interest! As a kid, I always imagined myself in the shoes of, say, the great Sundiata Keita, who established the Mali Empire, or the likes of Nzinga Mbemba in the Kongo Empire. I had always thought I would have been a great ruler, changing both the course and history of the slave trade. Hence, learning about Shaka Zulu, the Mfecane, and other struggles to build empires that were destroyed by colonizers captivated my fullest attention in class and I did extremely well in those tests. "Always think of Mtendele High School and students from Kamudzu International Secondary School whenever you are studying and doing your exam preparation," Mr. Chikazinga had said before he paused, most probably to let me digest what he had just uttered. These two schools he mentioned were just as good as LIBOSS and often had many top students in the national examinations. He allowed himself a few seconds before saying a highly encouraging statement:

"We all believe in you, and we also hold high expectations from you."

This talk made me feel proud of who I was, and, for once, I hid all my troubles. What could be more empowering than knowing that people believed in you? People such as your father, your teachers, those whom you looked up to.

During this period, I was happy and satisfied with life. But I also knew well that joy has a slender body that breaks too soon, as the African saying goes.

The thirteenth of July came sprinting by. I did not even realize that the term had just ended. There was a lot to follow, just like a lot had happened in that short twinkle.

Early in the morning, I felt a little anxious as to what the next step would be. This was my last day in Likuni. My last day in LIBOSS. It was hard to think about. Even worse, I was not allowed to tell anyone. But rules are there to be broken, aren't they?

I had told a couple of friends that I was leaving the school for good. On one of the Saturday outings, I had felt obliged to talk to three of my closest friends at least: Nifasha Elias, Emmanuel Konzaufe, and Leonard Munthali. We were in Chigwirizano when I broke the sorry tale and watched them shrink like heated ice. Chigwirizano was a small townlike location, the nearest shopping center from our school, and we often found ourselves there. It was out of bounds, and a few students were suspended for not having the patience to wait for the Saturday outing on the last Saturday of every month. Anyone who has ever lived in the imprisonment of boarding school knows that there is always a way, but that there are always consequences when one is caught, too. Some consequences were larger than others. LIBOSS, unlike many other schools, was both a government school and a missionary secondary school, and the combination did not tolerate any loose behavior. I had waited for this perfect moment when we were finally allowed out to tell my three best friends that I was leaving the school, never to return. I never told them where I was going. I never knew where I was going! I just knew that I was going.

On this last Friday of the term, I had woken up early to prepare myself for my journey back to Sangano. I ended up ruminating more on my time in this school, especially in the final term of the academic year. I reflected on the unfairness that was the students in Form 1 having to do all the manual work in the school, like cleaning and moving furniture, all year while all other forms just watched, helping only on special occasions. I was to have no pleasure standing like a king and watching subsequent "Form Ones" toil as temporary slaves. Many of us had been waiting for that day! James and the rest of the Form 4 students had had their graduation day sometime during the term. I had sat with him, taken pictures with him, and envied how cute all the graduates looked, let alone the care and respect that they were given. I would have no such pleasure! I was one of the brighter students, if not the brightest, and it was certain that I would have been the head boy or the librarian—the highest level of authority that a student at LIBOSS could get. This was a wasted dream.

I rolled in my bed, feeling a little blue and afraid, and I glanced at the photo album that I always kept next to my bed. I loved pictures. I started to browse through it, and the very first photo to appear was from May 17, 2012, when we were in the Maula Cathedral for vocation day. Poignant thoughts! I had lived as a Christian throughout my time at LIBOSS and had seen my spirituality grow exponentially. With friends, we had formed the "Pray without Ceasing" prayer group, which was renamed "Maria Divine Mercy" after my departure. I also sang in the school choir with the pretty girls from Likuni Girls Secondary School. Many more things had I done to please God and myself. On that vocation day, different Catholic schools had sent students to the cathedral in Lilongwe. I was among the lucky ones. A lot was expected from LIBOSS students—singing, behaving, devotion, and so on. I met almost all their expectations. I played the keyboard for the school choir with another

young keyboardist for St. Martin Choir at Likuni Parish—
our parish. I also talked to priests, thereby meeting most,
if not all, of the expectations on me. There was a German
priest too: "a messenger from Rome," as they had introduced him. I had never thought about Germany—or about
Germans— but I had often thought about Rome.

I had run into the priest who oversaw vocation for the
whole country, and inquired what it took to join the clergy.
The first step was to get into a seminary. For that, I had to
keep in touch. He kindly gave me his contact information,
which I felt was useless on the morning of the thirteenth
of July. In no time, I was to pack my bones and brush the
Malawian dust off my feet. Brother Michael from Likuni
Parish and Brother Chikwesa, the geography and life-skills
teacher who turned out to be my mentor, had accompanied
us there. The next photograph I saw was one taken with
them, which set me thinking about my teachers.

I would miss the teachers who were meanest yet most
influential: Mrs. Mzumara, my biology teacher, had been
the only teacher to punish me in my whole year at LIBOSS
by showing me where to slash grass when I failed to answer
a question in her class. I would also miss those who were
simply lovely, like Mrs. Kayange, the English teacher who
taught us poems with a smile, reading aloud and using
varying tones in a way that felt like we were in kindergarten
but offered a real learning experience. I would miss the
brainiest, like Mr. Tera, the agriculture teacher who never
took books with him. He was a retired university profes-
sor and always dictated his notes from his mind. I would
miss those who had supported me, like Mr. Chirwa with
his strong religious ideology, which he enforced in any

way possible while never pressuring anyone. He had once described his culture shock when he swam with completely naked people in Germany in the late seventies. He had used this story to introduce a talk about sexuality. I knew absolutely nothing about Germany then, other than it was a European country whose leaders had started the First and Second World Wars. Crazy Germans.

I tossed and turned every second, uncomfortably thinking about the many things that had gone wrong during my time at LIBOSS. For example, I had fallen sick during the term and had had to be dismissed, to be sent home to recover. I was taken to my father's friend in the capital as a stop on the way to my family. It was a hard and horrible experience, especially knowing that as I struggled with my unclear sickness others in school were advancing. I hated missing classes more than anything. A teacher once told me that in a minute of absence something valuable, or even the key to unlocking your fullest potential, could pass you by. I was less than ten then but the statement never escaped my mind, and remains locked into my grain-sized brain even now. The days I spent at "sick bed," the isolated building in the school compound near our hostels where every sick student would be quarantined; the pills I had to take at every meal that I either did not eat or ended up spewing; the unforeseen journey back to the camp as sick as I was and many more sad memories associated with the sickness haunted me. But it wasn't the worst experience.

I thought of the demonstrations that took place in our school terrain that had adverse effects on the students. A party called the United Democratic Front (UDF) was having a lot of fun in a most cynical way, dancing and dancing as a form of demonstration, and the government, led by the Democratic Progressive Party (DPP), intervened on the grounds that the UDF was having an unknown political meeting. We watched from the trees inside the school even as others climbed the brick wall that enclosed the school. Everything was so dramatic that we could not resist. Besides, the drama happened in our playground along the road that connects Chitsapu and Chigwirizano, the town centers nearest to our school. Who would have wanted to miss a free show? The police had come at the government's command, and they threw tear gas canisters amid the people singing, dancing, and praising their party leader, Atupele Muluzi. I watched people stumble while others ran and fell helplessly as the chaos broke out. Many failed to breathe. Many students—luckily no one was seriously injured—ran as fast as they could to the hostels to wash their faces. For some, it took a few minutes before they could breathe properly again with no problems, while for many others it took hours.

I remembered a wise man's comparison of politics to a dirty game with mostly dirty people driven by nothing but dirty minds. I hated politics as much as I loved change.

Soon all these would become memories. Memories for a lifetime. The good friends, the good education, the nature around, the church, even the intense feeling of hunger that usually led several students to find themselves out of bounds and facing the deputy.

I started filling the remaining space in my suitcase, feeling a surge of emotion, but I did not cry. The refugee life had dried all my tears. It was not the first time I had deserted those whom I loved and that which I was attached to! After all, my grandma's backyard and banana plantations, the various types of avocado and mango trees, and the hills and mountains of my homeland were now history to me.

Lost in my thoughts, I also thought of the friends I had made and whom I would miss. Those who mattered most to me were also those who often sought my advice and help in one way or another. I felt like a traitor to them. It was scary that soon I was to begin a new life altogether, and I had completely no idea what it would look like. Would the journey itself be as horrible as my trans-Tanzanian travels, when I spent three days without food and had the bag assigned to me, filled with the whole family's shoes, stolen while in Morogoro? Was the destination another refugee camp, again? What *was* the meaning of life?

It was time to run again, to run away from the broil that was slowly developing in Malawi, but for how long would we keep running? When would I find my fled freedom? I was so confused. All these questions had simply no answers. After a whole academic year in the best school in the country, a school I had desired and worked hard for; after a whole academic year as the best student, with much hope and aspirations for what my future hid, at the time, I had succumbed to my family's decision to move on. A lot happens when you are a minor. Even worse, when you are the youngest. You have no choice in whatever decisions are being made, and your mother still wants you to stick to her back.

This was my very last day as a student at Likuni Boys Secondary School.

I left the school around noon with a classmate who was heading in the same direction. He lived in Tsangano, while I was going to my father's shop a few kilometers ahead of him, in Sangano. It had taken the security workers at school a lot of time to search each student. They normally did this at the end of each term to control any outflow of school materials. Missionary schools!

This classmate and friend was very special to me. He was one of the few who trusted me utterly. He told me all his problems and asked me for advice from time to time. He was constantly accused of this or that, and he often sought my consolation. He was needy and from a very impoverished area and background and was always accused of theft. I never judged him. We would sit somewhere and pray before he tried to share his stress and anxiety with me. I valued his courage and his trust, and I hoped I helped him. I never told him that this was the last time he would see me. Just like I never told him how much worse of a background I came from.

We left the school together, reached the bus station and sat in a bus that took a century to fill up. When we finally drove off, I realized there was a pregnant lady who was standing. The Malawian bus conductors did not care whether there were seats or not; they just wanted money, even if that meant some passengers would have to stand for two hundred kilometers. I kindly offered her my seat, which meant two things: either I might regain a seat if enough passengers got off in the nearer towns along the route, or I would have to stand for the whole journey. It was a long distance from the capital in the center of the country to almost the south. My friend looked at me, and I could not tell whether it was a reaction of surprise or admiration on his face. Over time I had fathomed that I had grown to become his role model. He was not the only one. A few minutes into the journey, he also offered his seat to another elderly person. That was very encouraging to me. We did not speak a lot along the way, except when we reached town centers and I had to buy snacks or a drink. He dropped off at his station, and I proceeded on since mine was ahead. I do not remember hugging him to say goodbye, even though I knew he would never see me again! All I know is that I felt sad seeing him fade behind as the bus resumed the journey.

I felt lonely, and I was again dumped far away in my thoughts. I reached for a dilapidated phone that I had bought from James Chandamale and played the only song that it could contain. Its memory capacity was sixteen megabytes, so I had filled it with a few pictures and that one song that I got from a Rwandan friend. It was a song titled "Icyo Dupfana Kiruta Icyo Dupfa" by a Rwandan singer called Man Martin. It talked about peace and reconciliation, something that occupied my mind when I was not thinking about my own troubles. *Why don't we enact love and reject what divides us, in order to achieve peace? / Why should someone suffer because of where he was born though he never chose to be born there?* These lyrics were in Kinyarwanda, a language that I had learned to speak fluently from my numerous Rwandan friends, including Nifasha. Listening to this exacerbated my thoughts about my friends, the future of Malawi, and my homeland. I felt so nostalgic. I hated life.

Preoccupied by the music and my memories, I never heard the bus conductor announcing that we were in

Sangano. Around five kilometers later, I felt a bit uneasy. I did not remember what the station looked like. I inquired from the conductor how long it would take for us to get there, only to receive a look of utter disgust. I felt scared, and the words that followed scared me even more.

In fluent Chichewa, he said, "Spoiled kids like you are so busy plugging headphones in their ears that you do not even realize it when we announce the stations!" he paused and looked at me again, intently, then said, "We have already passed it!" I felt as if a thunderstorm had just struck. *Spoiled kids?* The two words resounded at the very back of my brain with an even greater intensity. I thought I knew the spoiled kids well. I did not know I could be classified under that category. Maybe I used to be one, back before we started embarking on these endless journeys; these quests for survival and freedom; these pursuits of the future, which we always lost our grip on, no matter how hard we tried to hold on. I was terribly confused and did not know what to ask, let alone express my helplessness with my poor Chichewa. I felt so daunted, knowing that this would be in my mind all the way back to Sangano. I had learned my lesson.

The bus dropped me off there and then, leaving me in the middle of nowhere. My homework was to get back to the station, and as a man I had to arrange that myself.

My father was waiting when I arrived. He received me with all the love the world could offer and fed me like a local farmer who has had an abundant harvest for the first time in years. He treated me like a king, making me feel at peace with the world.

A few days to go.

CHAPTER 3:

MIDNIGHT

In late August, 2012, we set out for the Kingdom of Swaziland. Known for its stability and peace—which I later realized was the result of the people's silence and their silenced voices in challenging politics—I thought it was the yearned-for path to freedom. It was instead an unprecedented way to intensified misery, at least for the next few days, weeks, and months. I soon wished I had known better while still in Malawi. Maybe I could have resisted my family's wish to get me out of what was "the best school" for me, out of my shortcut to a long-held dream. Away from the reputable boy I had become. But life should be left for what it is and what it will be!

While leaving Maputo, I felt like something was wrong. It was probably the resentment and apprehension I had resulting from the mutable life I lived. I had kept on believing that it would typically normalize the more experience one gained as an undocumented immigrant—or as part of the undesirable elite, those famous yet forgotten beings. The refugees. We had spent almost three years in Malawi. Life had begun to become *normal* and now here we were, crossing more borders—illegally! The fear was much more intense this time.

I thought of all the frontiers my family and I had crossed without any legal documents, just as most families fleeing their beloved countries did. Now that I was almost fifteen years old, with some geography from school, some knowledge about how the world worked, and having watched some news, thinking about all this had turned into a habit. Thinking about life was my *meditation*. "What were borders, anyway?" I constantly found myself wondering. They looked like lines, sometimes straight and sometimes confused. It had occurred to me as I observed the African map: Namibia and Angola; Mauritania and Chad. Some perpendicular lines separating nations and people. My heart ached a little bit! Even more, knowing that most of the conflicts that caused us to flee and claimed millions of lives, were the direct result of some men who sat around some table somewhere and drew those lines, driven by greed and power, unaware of where and whom they were dividing, made me more dejected. The mutability of my life was a direct consequence of those actions more than thirteen decades prior!

With each step toward the fence that separated Swaziland from Mozambique, running a few kilometers along the Lomahasha–Namaacha border, I thought more about my destiny and my purpose in life. I was young. A follower. My fate was my family. What if I had a choice? The lower my tracks kept going, the lower my hopes kept slipping, but I was with *hope*. I never lost her.

On this day, however, things were different. Apprehension got the better of me, especially because from time to time we would meet a Mozambican soldier or two. I remember vividly one instance that shook the hell out of us as we moved along the fence looking for the best spot to penetrate through. We passed under a tree—an acacia tree with majestic branches projecting radially over a large area. We had been walking for a while under the scorching sun with lots of luggage and no rest. My sister thought of resting for a while. She looked like fresh vegetable leaves that had just been exposed to very hot steam or put in boiling oil. We all did. As we deliberated whether resting was a good idea, we heard some voices. A fluent Portuguese that could not be sourced from anywhere around these parts.

We all were overwhelmed by shock and trepidation when we unanimously looked up, only for our eyes—all of our eyes—to lock onto those of the four soldiers chilling cheerlessly in those very branches. My parents rushed to withdraw theirs. I do not remember what came of mine or the others', but I know well that we immediately regained all the strength we needed in the world and slowly sauntered down the apparently unending path along the chain-link fence.

I still believe that whole family communicated, through extrasensory perception, that if the ground were kind enough to open up and swallow us, none of us would have objected. Nonetheless, it didn't. The two military men—or border patrol officers, whoever they were—were kind enough to ignore our presence. Our feet did what was best. We did not have a friendly past with soldiers, as you know! Especially soldiers in trees. I grew up surrounded by the tropical rainforests!

That same evening, we found ourselves in the Siteki police station. Siteki is a town in the Lubombo region of eastern Swaziland. That was as far a ride as we providentially got, having finally made it to the other side of the fence, and having walked almost the same distance opposite our initial direction to access the tar road that took us in.

I hated seeing my father acutely questioned despite his hunger, tiredness, and anxiety. The officer in civilian clothes who interrogated him, like a teacher would a dumb student refusing to speak up in his oral exam, was of medium height, stout and sturdy. He had distinct eyes, large and reddish, which did not fit with his round face. I observed him discreetly in the dimly lit police reception room. I despised his aggressive voice and look, both of which I successfully avoided. I couldn't be questioned because I was merely fifteen years old at the time.

Later, the police kindly offered us some sort of tasteless food and then showed us where to sleep. We spent the sleepless night in the corridors and walkways between the prison cells. That was my introduction to Swaziland. I resumed my *meditation* before I could search for sleep and eventually find it.

Waking up, we were offered some water and a different type of prepared food. The policewomen stationed for the night and half of the day that we spent there seemed nice. Looking at how sympathetically and kindheartedly they portrayed themselves, I wondered inwardly whether this geniality was anything but a façade. It was easy to lose faith in humanity.

Toward noon, when we were presumably all questioning whether we were prisoners instead of refugees, we got a directive to gather our things and come outside. Then we were searched. Not simply searched, but harshly scrutinized. Every pocket was turned out, every piece of paper read. When the scrutiny and the terror were over, we were still refugees—but not really refugees because we were stripped of our Malawian refugee status there and then, but more asylum seekers. A step backward!

Our next stop was Malindza Reception Center, also known as Mpaka Refugee Camp, in the town of Mpaka. We were transported in a police van and a compact car. I was privileged to have been in the car, from which I could look at the view outside. Despite the uneasiness that had reigned in all of us, I still enjoyed the journey down the Siteki hill, especially the part where I could view the naked valley stretching from Langa to Lonhlupheko and beyond. I also marveled at the fact that I could open the window a little bit and feel the breeze. I don't recall seeing much along the way because from time to time my mind retreated back to the car, and the journey was not as long as I had thought.

While in Mpaka Refugee Camp, the surroundings looked dirty yet fine. The camp management was expecting us: blankets, soap, and toilet paper were already evenly distributed along the cemented balcony of the offices. There were nine packs, one for each of my family members. We did not spend much time in the camp manager's office because in the coming days we were to do the daunting interview under both the police and the Ministry of Home Affairs, as well as the photoshoot. Everyone had to go through this to be officially declared an asylum seeker, and then they waited forever for the interviews that would grant or deny their refugee status. I quickly noticed that the UNHCR was either inactive or nonexistent in this so-called refugee camp, and months later my fears were confirmed.

We were then led to where we had to lay our heads for a few nights. It was a twenty-square-meter space that an already well-established refugee had been forced to volunteer for our occupancy. Along the fifty or so meters that we walked from the office to "Titanic," our new paradise, we were scanned by what seemed like two hundred curious eyes. Most were still young. They were excited, just a little! The older eyes that I managed to see all looked tired, sad, and dejected. I quickly realized with no doubt that life was poignant there. This epiphany was confirmed by Titanic itself, in addition to its filthy surroundings.

This Titanic was as large as the historical Titanic itself. It was a very long and wide concrete block warehouse building that hosted most of the refugees in the camp. A gigantic cuboid with an equally oversized triangular prism on top—the roof. From the outside it looked fine, and the walls seemed strong like the walls of Constantinople, although not as complex or intricate. It had a lot of ventilation spaces down below and on top, most of which had plastic bags stuck inside. I wondered why the residents had decided to block them. The iron sheets that served as the roof were possibly one of my everlasting memories of its exterior. When you looked at them under intense sunshine from a one-kilometer distance up the dusty road that led into the camp premises, they reflected much of the sunlight. This caused them to appear whitish and shiny, like clear water in a lake or sea, when observed from an appropriate angle around midday. By merely looking at them, virginal as they were, you would never associate them with the situation they shielded right beneath.

Inside, Titanic was a sorry sight. There was no ceiling. Four-meter-high concrete brick walls separated its numerous regions; the walls were possibly less than three quarters of the overall height of the building, with no ceiling. Below the roof was a web of illegal, irregular, and perilous electric cables. Individual family spaces were divided by either blankets (like those we received from the office) and thick plastic sheets or wooden planks and their variations for those who were rich enough. As old and dilapidated as these planks were, they looked awful.

In these "paradisial" premises were a lot of music lovers. Many *musics.* As weird as it sounds, every corner possessed a loud speaker set playing songs of every nature. Congolese rumba, Somalian folklore, Rihanna's newest release, the Burundian *Inanga,* and many more unidentified cross-cultural genres. All playing loudly and at once. There was no ceiling, and the blankets and plastic sheets that separated families and rooms reflected so much sound that all the noise added together was simply sickening and traumatizing. Added to this were the people watching movies, parents—especially mothers—shouting at their children,

children crying after having been severely thrashed for all sorts of reasons, as well as husbands and wives beating each other up. It was all traumatizing.

Day and night, night and day, this was the situation we encountered. Then it got better, because we got used to it. We got used to the trauma as time went by.

My first "blissful" night in the Malindza reception center was extremely melancholic. The weather on its own, both dry and hot, was dreary and depressing. The darkness was dark enough that both my heart and soul could feel it. The very same evening we arrived, some people tried to be nice to us. A girl helped clean up the section we had been given to sleep in. With the help of her mother, she swept and mopped the floor. The floor was partly cemented, made of huge concrete square blocks that were lacking in some parts. This was a good gesture. Another family brought us a carpet on which we could lay our heads. This was a very nice gesture too. In all our desolation, we did not speak much. We did not want to speak much. But we thanked them.

Again, many eyes passed by. Some entered through a now nonexistent door that used to open onto the lower-right wing of the Titanic that we had been put in, seemingly to see their friends yet always with the intention of taking a glance at us; others peeped through the ventilation holes that were all over the walls, some inbuilt while others created by wind and time through a process of destruction. Some who were kinder came to try to make us talk. Like many refugees, and especially many of those who led refugees, they had no value to add to our situation. Except the feeling that we had no one, no privacy, and no future.

We sat in that corner with much sympathy, sadness, and confusion for the rest of the evening. We were like people sitting around a fresh, poverty-stricken widow; the only difference was that we embodied her in many ways.

Toward seven o'clock the same evening, it was time for me to expel the nutritious, tasteless elements I had been provided by the police the night and day before. Even that was a huge problem. The first person whom I approached, a Congolese, told me frankly that his family did not own a toilet. I was confused. He pointed at someone whom I could approach. I was soon to know that for all the families that lived in that hell-like place, there were only fourteen toilet rooms, thirteen of which were owned by fewer than twenty families, and just one was shared by the rest of the people living in the camp. That was life.

I borrowed the key from the family he had pointed to and enthusiastically hastened. I did not even take time to listen properly as she explained the specific toilet door number that I had to look for, or the specifics about the use of that latrine. That had its effects. When I arrived, I had to try the key to every lock. The very first door was the common one, I guessed, and soon confirmed my hunch: it was open and had shit all over. I wondered where people stood. The third door was the right one, and it was a bit cleaner. I sat very comfortably, did all the "work" with ease, reminiscing about the good old days when we had built our own pit latrine, which we shared with no one and cared for so much. But when it was time to do the "after-work," my mouth slowly opened in utter surprise because of all the things that were wrong. Let alone the fact that there was no toilet paper—that was a private issue—the toilets were very old and dilapidated. I was convinced that they were the best when they had first come into use. They were flush toilets with white ceramic seats as usual, embedded tranquilly in box-like structures measuring a square meter—rooms with iron-sheet roofs. Having seen years of exposure and use, however, they had slowly disintegrated. The only remaining bits were the actual holes and the ceramic seats. All the steel pipes that carried water were no longer working; all that remained were the parts inserted into the walls. Consequently, there was no water to flush my waste with! I learned the hard way that anyone who wanted to use these private rooms must bring along water in a bucket to flush the deed. The good Samaritan who gave me the key had not explained this—or maybe she had but I had not listened, or else she had assumed I knew. Either way, I found myself in that situation. My family had just arrived; we had no water and no bucket.

At night, Cindy, the eldest of a family of five headed by a child, cooked for us. They served us rice and cabbage. It was tasty but spare. Of all the families in that small refugee camp, some orphans saw to it that we ate something, not only for that night but also for the ensuing nights as we struggled to live. I learned about their kind hearts and who they were, and I thanked God for the life we possessed! As time passed, they became dearest and nearest to us.

When it was time to sleep, my heart was completely torn to pieces. Only time and prayer put the fragments back together. That night was the first and only time that all nine members of my family were lined up, from my father to his granddaughters, my nieces, on the same floor: an arrangement that lasted a few days, had never happened before and never happened again. On the carpet. Covered by the blankets we had been offered that afternoon. I did not sleep; I *meditated*. Thinking about this engraved an image into my mind that will die only when I do. It is a constant reminder of my refugee life experiences each time I lay my back in any comfort now. It is a stain on my heart yet a source of strength, because it is the last thing I want my children and their great-grandchildren to experience.

The next morning, we were hesitantly woken up by some weird noise that sounded like a horn or trumpet or something in between, and the chaotic noise of children screaming "Pakela, pakela!" These kids were so loud that, alarmed, we all rose and sat up as quickly as possible. I searched from the back of my head what *pakela* meant; was it Swahili? Kirundi? Chichewa? Crap, I was no longer in Malawi! I tried to force a smile. I didn't even know what the local language was called, except that the greeting was "Sam-bon-ane" which later turned into "Sawubona" and "Sanibonani." Perhaps *pakela* was a word in the local language?

I was correct! The vice camp manager who had received us the previous day, a very fierce, tall, ageing lady who rarely smiled and had a perpetual angry look, had talked about *pakela*.

"For the first three months that you are in Malindza Reception Center," she had said before pausing, staring at the nodding adults to put a slight emphasis on the "Reception Center" part, "you are provided with a morning porridge and lunch every day. All those who are eighteen years and above stop getting this after three months, because we assume you are now used to the camp and you can provide for yourselves." She stopped for a while, and I saw my father cringe although he tried not to show it. Then seconds later, "Oh, unless of course you are in school, then the kitchen can continue taking care of you." Good that I was *hopefully* going to school. Too bad there was no evening meal!

Pakela was a siSwati word for "receive," and the children used it to indicate their excitement to "receive" their share of food of the morning or afternoon. Normally, one of the kitchen workers blew the vuvuzela to indicate that it was time, then young kids and young adults alike raced down the open area between the not-so-good-looking old refugee houses and the-very-good-looking staff houses and kitchen.

Frankly, I enjoyed the porridge in the morning. In fact, I would have loved to have all of the less-than-two-liters that our whole family of nine was provided, but of course we were in destitution together as a family! For lunch, from the first day onward, the bitter-looking, bitter-tasting vegetables we got were thrown away the very same way they came, except for a spoonful or two that was accidentally eaten for tasting, out of hunger and curiosity! These vegetables came along with a form of *ugali,* some hardened pop that surely would be better. While most of the family complained of lack of appetite, a significant part of this ended up in my stomach and that of my brother with the help of some salty water from our new neighbors. And that was just how it was!

We were provided with only breakfast and lunch, but what of the evening meal? My father did not have any money left after spending the little he had crossed with from Malawi on the journey, the smuggler, and basic transit needs. Even if he had, we knew nothing about where to get what and had to start all over. The idea that our evening meal was being taken care of by some random orphans clearly seemed to make matters worse. At least for my parents, whose brains came before their stomachs.

On our second day, I observed the sadness and gloom that imprisoned the whole family. Then I turned to the Almighty, an act my parents had taught me well. I proposed that we have a prayer every day at three in the afternoon, that being the hour of Divine Mercy. My parents received the proposal with both hands, with their hearts and souls. My siblings did not bother! They were very determined to be depressed, and they were quite successful. They could sit for anywhere for minutes and hours, silently, staring at the floor or at the roof, with disconsolate faces. Then, as we started making sense of people and life, they started roaming into neighbors' houses trying to watch television, sometimes disregarding the sleeping hours of the neighbors or even their privacy.

The family seemed to talk less and less, such that the loud silence became a melodious tune, a chorus that accompanied our sleepless nights. Then anger seemed to possess some of my siblings, even in answering the simplest questions from my parents like "Where have you been?" or "What do you think we shall do next?"

I had enough time to *meditate*, to figure out how my life was evolving, especially in terms of my education. I had always wanted to embark on that educational journey but every time I thought I had leeway, the winds were strong enough to press me down. I had faith and all it took but no wings to fly with. Even my running, let alone flying, had been ambushed by life itself. I had to succumb to the family's wishes and trail behind them, my dreams limping.

But I was determined. I was determined to walk or crawl, whatever it took! I knew every story has an ending: tragic for the unfortunate characters and joyous for those who adhere to the will of the writer. I was the protagonist in my own story, just like in this one.

Since our arrival, the weather had been acting weirdly. The woeful winds blowing under the scorching sun exchanged dust for rain from time to time during the day. During the night extreme heat or cold, depending on how the day had been, seized chances to trouble the troubled. Sometimes in my struggle to sleep I could feel the swaying trees echoing gloom as I tossed and turned under the light blanket, between my two brothers on the plain carpet. The cold could infiltrate through all the holes of the Titanic, which was inevitable no matter how many people tried to stick plastic sheets in the holes. Soon rain would follow the cold's footsteps, and we would find ourselves unable to sleep because, to add to the traumatizing life we lived, the roof did not help but instead leaked as if carefully monitored. Each day took us from worse to worse.

I prayed and believed. Then *prayed* and believed. And after that, I prayed and thanked.

After two weeks, our prayers to both God and the camp management were answered. We were shown a large section of the other end of Titanic that we were to occupy. That was good news, but a lot of effort was required to clean it up and build it however we wanted.

Cleaning went as easily as one might expect. After all, it was tons of human excreta we were supposed to remove along with many dangerous rusty metals and other types of rubbish that we didn't know how to dispose of. It was as if there were no people living next to that area, for in my perspective, it was the fifteenth toilet and the camp's waste disposal. We had to kill a few snakes too; this we did not tell my mother and my eldest sister due to their fear of snakes.

A lady who, together with her daughter, had helped us clean up the first place we were temporarily occupying heard that we were soon to relocate to the other lower wing of Titanic. She leaked to my father the place from which we were to cut trees to build our shelter. The afternoon after the cleanup, we, the males of the household, set out to that place under her guidance. The following few days were laborious as we cut and carried the few saplings we were to use as bases for separating the rooms. We had to brave the sun and the snakes, both of which proved to be daunting. On the very first day we killed two adult black mambas, among the most dangerous snakes around and widespread in southern Africa. All that followed were stories!

Slowly but surely, we faced the harsh realities as men. We still had no stove and no toilet to use, but we were getting there. Having a section of our own was a start to self-dependence and a creation of freedom. The free freedom we all deserved! *Freedom?*

CHAPTER 4:

DREAMS

I sat down feeling bad about myself. This was not exactly the place I had imagined when I left Malawi. The place stank, a very strong and strange stench. A foul smell trapped in the dark, nauseating blankets that sheltered almost everyone living in Titanic diffused to the outside. And when met with the poop of babies everywhere, the rubbish dumped all around, and finally the toilets that were not far away from Titanic, it produced a strong, strange smell. This was complemented by gases diffusing out of the digestive tracts of the hundreds of sleepers in the Titanic.

This morning I got tired of rolling on the rough surface of the cartons that unwillingly lay on the tree branches we had carefully put together and raised about forty centimeters off the floor to act as a bed for my elder brother and me. We did not have a mattress, and on top of these cartons we put two or three dilapidated blankets, some of which had been given up by their owners after serving them for ages. As a result, our backs complained from time to time, especially if sleep played tricks on us and evaded our attempts to own it for most of the night. I woke up begrudgingly early and decided to sit outside.

I looked around me: there was no one. It was still before the cock's crow, so I guessed people were still deep in their slumber, including those who were going to school themselves. No one stirred. No one but a few lazy houseflies that seemed to like so much the hovering, disgusting odor.

Nature often communicates. It was the first time I saw a housefly in this, my newest home. You always need small indicators to take you to the far land where you wished to be. Thanks to these houseflies, I found myself thinking of how common they were back home, and how we used to play around with them. They were very common. Especially if people had wounds or bruises from all sorts of causes: war, violence, disease, and so on. They could feast on the reddish blood or the oozing pus of the victims. The latter was the best for them, I had always thought!

Houseflies would come buzzing, grateful for the attractive smelly liquids. They knew better than to land on a conscious person because if they did they either died or escaped without really enjoying what they had pursued. Oftentimes there were a lot of corpses anyway—some freshly lying around in the open, some hidden deep in the bushes—so they had no reason to pay their frequent visits to other living creatures, I used to think. But I guess they were called "houseflies" for a reason since a house is never occupied by cadavers. Unless you were really dead inside, which seemed to be the case in the refugee camps.

As kids, we had a lot of fun with the houseflies. We pretended not to take notice of them as they elegantly danced their way toward us, then the moment they landed on our contusions—especially if we still had two hands—we killed them with just one clap. Then we amused ourselves by observing the sticky semisolid stuff that came out of their boneless bodies. I enjoyed the process, especially when I competed with my friends to see who killed the most flies.

But here, it was a bit different. I was all alone and with no wounds, luckily. Yes, they followed the stench, but I was still a little bit puzzled. Back in the day the houseflies came around noon or during the day. They buzzed around when the unforgiving sun either caressed the gentle skin or scorched the hell out of the basking bastards. I could not recall ever seeing any housefly in the early morning. Maybe because back then I slept soundly regardless of the background music of guns and grenades. Maybe because I was still way too young to take notice of these things? Maybe because it was only in those times that I had freely basked in the sun, often with friends. Even in Malawi, I remembered, the houseflies only came out in the sun although it was way too windy and dry for them to have any significant numbers flying around. Swaziland was even drier, yet here they were.

I looked at those early morning houseflies and remembered that back home, they could fly around freely even though we killed them. Here they seemed to be trapped in some coldness that froze their muscles, assuming they had any, and that prevented them from jumping around and flying around. They looked disgusting too, now that I was starting to notice things.

Looking at these nauseating houseflies as the stench grew stronger and stronger, I felt like I should go back to my so-called bed and give sleep a second attempt. I had not slept for the entire night, because I often found myself in many strange thoughts. *Meditating*. And this was exactly what happened: I thought about houseflies, wondering what their use for humanity was, if any. Nonetheless, I went back to my so-called "bed." Before I finally fell asleep, I concluded that human lives were as good as those of houseflies. I convinced myself of this epiphany. Later, I would pin down the actual relationship between the two.

The initiation phase had been completed. The police had come, we had been officially declared asylum seekers, and it was time to plunge ourselves into more pressing—or more depressing—problems. My father's was finance; my mother's medication for her frail and failing health. Mine was school. School was mine.

I could sit in the misery and think of my dear left-behind LIBOSS. In the mornings, I observed primary-school children from the camp in their shabby green-and-white (more brownish than white) uniforms or the high school teens seizing their bags while in black-and-white uniform, their feet in shiny or not-so-shiny black shoes, and my exasperation enhanced. To think about it, I needed school more than I ever did. I had left a missionary school behind me. I wanted to be in a missionary school.

Zoph, may God bless her soul, had been our closest family friend. Like Cindy, she knew every angle of our toils and troubles. A very beautiful and wonderful young lady, as selfless as the sun despite her own struggles as the head of her family, she always made efforts to meet our needs. I often wonder whether we could have survived the cruelty of life in Mpaka without their interventions. Once she understood my needs, she suggested places I could go to. Caritas Internationalis (Caritas), a Catholic organization that partnered with the Swazi Ministry of Home Affairs and the (absent) UNHCR to make a trio that presumably supported the refugees, was a good place to start. She was a very recent high school graduate and Caritas had paid her high school fees. Her younger brother and both her younger sisters were still in school, too.

I started enquiring more about the possibilities of getting Caritas to help me get to a Catholic school, but all my efforts were in vain. From time to time, different officials from the Ministry of Home Affairs visited the camp to supervise the labor we were doing, and I tried to interact with them about my issue. They said they would let me know when the time was right, but none knew any missionary schools.

Eventually, Zoph brought some delightful tidings: the Salesians of Don Bosco. It was the perfect match—another Likuni Boys Secondary school for me. It was a boys' high school situated in Manzini, the financial capital of Swaziland.

We did all that was required and finally got there to interact with the head of the school. My father and I were dressed in the best we had in hopes of treading taller than we were. When we managed to get hold of the principal, my conversation with him was very friendly and … well, not up to scratch. The first stab was knowing that it was not a boarding school, that even if I were admitted, I had to either commute the fifty kilometers from Mpaka to Manzini every single day or find some accommodation somewhere in Manzini. I might as well have forgotten about the LIBOSS in Manzini.

I understood well that until that moment my family and I still depended on the goodwill of other people, and it was faith that had brought me to request a place there. But something else evolved, just as the old adage that everything happens for a reason would have predicted.

When I left Malawi, I had completed my first year of high school. While primary school in Malawi is eight years long, in Swaziland it takes seven years; so my first year of high school in Malawi (Form 1) converts to the second year of high school in Swaziland (Form 2). I had been warned that if I did not want to repeat Form 2 then I had to go straight to Form 4. Explaining this to an experienced educator seemed implausible. Then, my fear transpired!

"So, you completed Form 2 as the best student," Petros, the principal of Salesians of Don Bosco, inquired. "And you would like to ensue to Form 4?"

"Yes," I answered.

"You know very well we have junior certificate examinations in Form 3?"

"Yes!"

"And that incorporates the contents from Form 1, Form 2, and Form 3?"

"Yes!?"

"And, by the way, how come your school report, as outstanding as it looks, shows that you completed Form 1 …?"

"Well, sir," I cut him off to explain my case, but he did not give me a chance.

A series of questions were posed to me. The dialogue seemed unidirectional. More questions toward me, all calm and friendly. I was too honest. I thought my self-confidence, which shrank by half after each query, could give me a place there. Besides, who lies when seeking a place in a missionary school? Little did I think about the world, the world that still rotates on its own axis, and how it remains a fact no matter how confident we can be about that not being the case.

In the end, I was given a choice.

"My friend, if you need a place here, I will have to put you in Form 2, and if you do extremely well in the first few weeks we are going to transfer you to Form 4. Meanwhile, if you really consider joining us, as you seem perfectly suitable for our school from what the school reports from your previous school demonstrate, your father should be looking for a place where you can stay somewhere in Manzini. Please go home and think about it!"

That was the closing statement. Still with all the calmness in the world.

I felt all the cyclones from the Far East rushing through my developing brain as I contemplated the offer. I descended the stairs from the administration block and walked slowly, making my way up to the Our Lady of Assumption Cathedral face to face with Caritas. I did not utter a word to my father since I was still digesting that most recent conversation with the principal. That was where all my brain energy and hormones, if any, were concentrated: to accept the offer or call it a diplomatic refusal.

That was the only Catholic missionary school in Swaziland that I had approached. I had heard of St. Michaels as well, an evangelical missionary school situated somewhere in Manzini, but that was a girls' school. *History!* After that, I did not endeavor to look for others, assuming they were there! But I became wiser. Whatever does not kill you makes you a man. I was not sure how much killing would be involved here, but I had heard of the killing of dreams. Slaughtering dreams—like slaughtering pigs right from the pigsty while they were still covered in their scrap. Or crap.

Before we realized it, my elder brother and I had started working for the authorities in those days. There were what seemed to be developmental projects—a pit latrine that needed to be built behind the clinic, that was all—that needed manpower. All the youth were going to school by then. All the men were deep into their thoughts, most probably contemplating the purpose of life, especially in those situations. The rest who were there and who felt comfortable talking to us gave us some reasons why they wouldn't work for the camp leaders: those in power were greedy; they were never truthful about the budgets and never fulfilled their promises, especially when it came to money; they looked down on those whom they used and did not serve those who they were meant to. All these were theories, some all of which were soon proved to be true.

My brother and I were the only hopeless characters who, innocently and out of pure respect, dedicated our time to the works taking place in the camp. The pit latrine was to be used by the clinic goers. Who wouldn't have liked to help?

This was community service for me, a way of paying back those who had received me. It was a way of appreciating the free *pakela* that I was getting, the shelter (though in shambles), but more important, the safety for my family. It was a way of connecting to people, especially my superiors, for I knew I had to sow this little grain, for it was just time, and then time would turn back. After all, I had nothing to lose except a few days of not *meditating*!

One of those good days, the camp manager came to see where we were working, either to appreciate our efforts or to see what she could report. Unlike the vice camp manager, a very fierce, tall, ageing lady who rarely smiled and had a perpetual angry look, the camp manager was short. Much shorter and older. She smiled every so often and seemed friendlier, although her mood swings were also something I soon came to accept. She was frail and never hesitated to ask for help, even if it was to get her a pen thirty centimeters away from her hand on the same table she was sitting at, while she could have simply bent and pulled it toward herself. I wondered whether she did that in the official meetings as well, or just when she was surrounded by the "very obedient" refugees.

She came to the workplace nicely dressed, in her red high heel shoes that significantly improved her height and exaggerated her graceful look. We were digging a pit in the garden, eight or ten meters away from the administrative building, and mixing cement in the same vicinity. We had spilt a lot of water in the process, and the soil around that area was wet but not noticeably wet. The poor old butterfly did not realize that until she stepped into and sunk in that soil, as I deduced from her facial expression, excited tone, and smallish showy red shoes covered with shit-like mud.

My immediate reaction was to approach her, take her out of the mud, and clean up her shoes. I displaced one of the rectangular concrete blocks on the usage waiting list and put it nearby for her to stand on; then calmly and thoughtfully genuflected, taking the shoes off her feet and shining them with the tap water we used to mix cement.

I did not look up to see the progressive changes on her face (as was gossiped about, later). Neither did I detect any changes in her tone as she watched me intently and silently, probably wondering what roots I sprouted from or what heaven had sent me down to hell, but I knew she was mesmerized and happy. Her "Ngiyabonga mtfwana wami" ("thank you my child") at that moment turned into a long-lasting relationship. The humble gesture did its magic, *uchawi!*

The manual work in the camp proceeded with stress after stress. Other than working on construction "projects," it was also common for us to move things around: from the office to the kitchen, from the storage to the office, from somewhere to the cars of the staff. Some of these things like clothes or notebooks that never complained for being shipped out of the camp were often designated for refugees.

I did not stop to envy those who went to school. Luckily, soon enough I found a best friend: my eldest brother's guitar became the best and only friend I had. He had bought it during one of those endless journeys and was very angry that the guitar and I were growing closer and closer because I had refused to help him carry it when we left Malawi. His anger was justified: if you were a parent, having dutifully raised a beautiful daughter right from the start, against all odds, and a seemingly crooked guy wants to get all the benefits of your pains, it would be considerably infuriating! But guys have their own ways. The guitar and I became even closer despite the quarrels with my brother from time to time, and then he let it go. He seemed too depressed to play it anyway!

I improvised, note by note, inscribing the melodious vibration into both my mind and heart, waiting for the day when my sighs of sorrow would be heard by the world. My former experience as a choir member and a keyboardist contributed to the delight I had, even though the guitar strings were as detuned as my voice itself, and I had no idea how to tune them! It was stress relieving, so fulfilling that whenever my system was down, whenever there was a blackout in my mind and soul, the guitar became my addiction rather than cigarettes and marijuana. I was later to realize that it was a therapeutic talent in progress, and I would have to thank myself for having allowed it to grow.

Time and again I rubbed shoulders with snakes, birds, and tiny insects while rummaging for a place to sit in the bushes, in the middle of nowhere, right outside the refugee camp. These were the days when I had to seek solace from the consoling creation of nature. And music. Both were handy, counteracting my ever-growing nostalgia for past times in my home country, in Dzaleka, and later at LIBOSS. Both protected me from the harsh reality of being lonely, even though my thoughts often fled from me to land right in the middle of Dzaleka Refugee Camp.

Time after time, my thoughts hailed Alberto for the friendship and brotherhood I greatly missed: praying, playing, and preying on life. I always thought of his sad, cheerless look when I left for LIBOSS. We had both deemed I was going for only a term—three months—and then I would come back for the vacation. I would then go again for another term and come back for the next vacation. And repeat. And repeat. Little did we know that as man proposes, God disposes. Little did we know that I would go to school for a term (while he worked his ass off to be admitted to LIBOSS as well, being in Grade 8 at the time), then to Sangano—to my father—for vacation. And repeat. And repeat. Then instead of repeating, as was my strong, sole desire, I would leave Malawi. Little did we know our paths would diverge then. *Maybe forever!*

Luckily, I was able to visit the camp on special occasions like Easter, when we had the adults' choir celebrate their anniversary; and when the Dominiko Savio choir celebrated the feast of its patron saint, Dominic Savio, in May; or on December 8 when our Catholic community in the camp put up a feast in honor of the Immaculate Conception, and such similar feasts.

Alberto and I would hug each other intimately and talk about stuff. School, friends, girls. Church, choir, spirituality. This was particularly important because we remained close and grew closer, in fact, during the period when he faded away and everyone looked down on him. Just in time, somehow, the Holy Spirit had managed (through others and me) to convince him to galvanize, reenergize, resuscitate himself, and return to his position in church. He rejoined the choir and proceeded with his duties as an altar boy and a reader during services. And everyone was happy! Quite funny how one becomes talked about when one drifts from people's expectations slightly, even if there were nothing spiritually fatal about it.

I was sure Alberto had missed me too. Missed the chit-chats and tittle-tattles that he could not obtain from anyone else, because even though he had many friends, we were each different and unique to him.

"You see, Michael," he said one day, preferring "Michael" to "John" or "brother," "There is something you should know about me."

"I'm listening," I said, not necessarily meaning it.

"I have a lot of friends. Different friends."

"Like everyone else, I guess."

"Not really." He liked saying that! "I mean, most of the time people befriend those whom they have a lot in common with—personality-wise, or those whose interests match." I could not tell where he was heading, but so long as he kept going, I was sure he would arrive somewhere significant. This was always the case. He continued, "I have you, very spiritual and intelligent in class and smart and ..."

"Stop!" I cut him off. I knew his rambling, especially when he was in the right mood.

"Anyway, then I have others like the Cash Money guys and the G-Unit ..." *As if they do not have names*, I made to interject, but suppressed it. "... whom you would really say they are the exact opposite of you, judging from what they do in the dark." I was beginning to gain a bit of interest.

My eyes widened and I stared at him keenly, more like an alert dog stiffly raising its ears and tail.

"What are you trying to insinuate?" *Insinuate.* I had heard or read that word somewhere; I didn't remember. There was no better time to practice your growing English vocabulary than when you were with your best friends. Not in class, because you got looked at. Not in the mirror—it felt weird, and you would have been lucky to have one, too. Best friends do not judge; they ignore and get motivated. Sometimes! We had decided to talk to each other more in English as a way of increasing our language ability—to add to those we already possessed.

"You and your big words!" was all Alberto said. Then he continued his discourse. "Well, I can give you more examples of different kinds of friends I have, but let's take just these two extremes for now."

"Yeah." *Yeah* was another English word I had learned from American English but also borrowed from German—another creepy language, I had heard.

"When you are close to people with different caliber, composure, and mental agility, you get a good overview of life. You learn a lot from different parties and you decide which parts you'd like to take, or who you'd like to be." Needless to say, I had long comprehended his point. But he proceeded before I even had a chance to pick up on that, probably exclaiming another big word from the new Oxford English Dictionary I had borrowed from the camp library, like *brilliant, superb,* or *splendid.* "There is a lot more to life that we don't get to know or experience because we enslave ourselves or channel our loyalty to only those whom look alike, think alike, live alike, love alike, laugh alike ..."

"Hmmm, that's quite true! [pause] I'm glad to have you, buddy. I can't imagine myself without you."

"Hey, that's my idea. My feeling, don't steal it. You!"

"No, it's mine."

"It's mine."

"No."

More than 2,155 kilometers away from him, I had to constantly battle these thoughts. They made me feel weaker, smaller, and incapable of orienting my own life. Choosing where to be and when to be there. Maybe if I were a bird, I could fly those kilometers and visit him and all my other friends, possibly continuing northward to the African Great Lakes to see both my family and my childhood surroundings: to the land where I knew well I could only be in thoughts and not in actual reality. I mean, how cool would it have been just to be there or anywhere I wanted to be? To see anyone I longed to see without being smuggled across borders not knowing whether I would see the light at the end of the … bush?

I was not a bird, though. I was a refugee caught in the mesh of life. The farthest distance I could go was to the bushes next to the camp. There I had some quietness, which I broke with the detuned guitar strings that prevented me from thinking and gave me some sense of realism. Music and nature were my inherent remedies.

Soon came what was possibly the most important recurring day of my life. The first of November. All Saints' Day. The day on which I came into this world.

Over the previous three years, I had gotten used to celebrating it together with Alberto. First with a prayer, and then (depending on whether luck had fallen from the sky or from nowhere) by buying some biscuits and a fizzy drink to share together. The two of us. We were born on the same day, same month, and same year. Only a few hours in between, which we always neglected except when it came to food. I always made sure that I left the last spoonful or two for him. Traditionally an older child eating from the same plate as a younger one must leave a mouthful for the younger one. Doing this made me feel more adult than he, and hence more powerful, stronger, and smarter (sometimes). And then, in his attempt to tease me, he would say that this was the reason why I kept growing like a toothpick, as slender as a cat's elbow. We would laugh and enjoy the love.

On November 1, 2012, my father bought *fusion*—too much of a strain on his financial capacity—a type of concentrated juice that gave eight liters to the one when you diluted it properly. Water problems in the camp! He had possibly forgotten. Still, it was nice to sit together as a family, with a few young individuals whom I had started to befriend, and enjoy the short, sweet taste.

Alberto was missing. I missed Alberto.

I prayed for myself and for Alberto. I bet he did the same! I forgot to ask afterward, but this was our tradition. Me and him. Him and me.

October and November came with their own struggles. Ever since we stepped into that Refugee Camp, the availability of water was always fluctuating. Come November, it was at its worst. The general feeling was that sometimes the management would intentionally block the salty water we had from reaching the camp. When asked, they would give all sorts of reasons as to why there was no water. The pipes had burst after being stepped on by wandering cattle; the machine pumping the water from under the ground was broken; there was a leakage here and there. Or something along those lines.

When we asked them to deliver the clean tanks of water available in the camp that came all the way from Siteki, their direct response was, "It is only for use in the kitchen"—for them to cook us *pakela* with. Such kindness!

We eventually had to move out of our comfort zones from time to time to look for water; to look for life. As the saying goes, "every dumping site has iron"; these were my first days exploring the premises around the camp

One of the places I got to see for the first time, which we later frequented to fetch water that we were sometimes denied, was Mpaka High School—my school to be. The school compound was located within half a kilometer west (or toward upper side) of the camp. You could see the fence and the storehouses, but the actual school buildings were a bit farther than that. You had to walk out of the camp and follow the main route to the Mpaka shopping complex until the main gate, where the route bent at ninety degrees to the right to join the main tar road five hundred meters or so away. Then you had to get on the left and walk two hundred more meters to get into the school. This longer access route to the school made it slightly harder to fetch water from there.

From time to time, we found ourselves emptying the borehole along the main street at Mpaka shopping complex. Pushing a wheelbarrow with seventy-five liters of water in containers at least twice a day, three or four times a week, soon became unbearable. Those who did not have friends from whom to borrow this useful transportation tool toddled around with twenty- or twenty-five-liter containers. If one were male, carrying two of these, one in each hand, would be easy. If one were female, then carrying one container was always the best option assuming one possessed a strong skull. Then the two or three kilometers, depending on where you fetched water from: an inevitable distance.

My elder brother and I were the ones responsible for fetching water. We often went together or took turns. These were the times when I started socializing with other equally miserable young people and got to know different individuals. We had to work together, hence we communicated from time to time about where the most suitable place to get water was. It was not uncommon that one or two Swazis would feel the urge to block us from fetching at some places, like at school. And this normally happened when one or two Swazis were selling water elsewhere.

Every single day had its own struggles, but the lack of water marked one of the hardest obstacles we had to overcome.

Each time the camp administration or the kitchen department unwillingly stretched out their hands to give water to the refugees, there were fights or heightened confrontations and insults. The Somalians and the Congolese were mostly at the forefront of these; the Burundians followed suit, and to a much lesser extent, the Rwandans. This observation always amused me! We had to form lines using the water containers we had. However, some people thought themselves bigger, or rather much more important, than others. Other people thought themselves cleverer. The world says, "first come first served," but we often mistook this statement to mean "most cunning most served," or "most arrogant most served."

There were situations when one person would hold up the line to fetch for five different families. It made me wonder why we complained about the amazing corruption and wonderful political instability that had shaken our countries to the core. This micropractice led to larger conflicts, often resulting in intercommunity tensions within the camp (with communities organized around nationalities).

There were also times when people would simply forcefully take over the fetching, regardless of who was fetching or whose turn it was according to the order of arrival or the line formed. This mostly resulted in fights.

Those who were supposed to help calm these down mostly chose not to interfere, and it made complete sense. If you were living peacefully, working peacefully, securing the salary that the government gave you, those fools could fight! They had been fighting anyway; that was why they were there. But another element was embedded deep within too: fear. You did not want to be caught in the middle of disputes between people who spoke languages you did not understand. Let them insult each other; things were what they were and would be what they would be.

In striving for positivity, I wanted to view all these struggles and indifferences as situations set before me to learn from and that would direct me to my destiny. I loved peace. I wanted peace. I always saw the routes I should never take in my life.

Consequently, my desire to be back in school increased exponentially. I started to develop visions of seeing the youth united. I have always been that guy on an island who tries to be different from the people around him, given that all around him is amiss. And here I was.

It pained me to see the young and old fight for water, a basic human resource. But I remained hopeful for the future.

Once more the place became lively. Livelier than I had imagined it could ever be. It became miserably vivacious. Schools were on break, and the daunting quietness was broken by those dismal, returning schoolgoers. Chit-chat seemed to be the only leisure in that gloomy despondency. When it came to numbers of people, the camp itself was as old as it was young, but during school breaks the young took over. This December break, especially, was filled with excitement because soon there would be the Christmas and New Year festivals, and on with life the circle of despondency would go. Beautiful juvenile smiles periodically hopped hopelessly and helplessly from house to house, like caged birds flapping their disabled wings to propel them as they jumped from one corner of their misery to another. This was golden proof of their innocent ignorance about the alternatives to such a circle of life.

I started making friends, although I made fewer new friends since there was a group I had already identified as appropriate for me. With most of those I befriended, we talked about nothing but their experiences in school. I continued to bury myself in books. Days came and went, and soon enough it was time for Mpaka High School to interview the prospective students—yet another opportunity to practice my skill at lying.

The camp management notified us of the interview. In fact, for some reason, the camp manager herself called me to her office, told me about it personally, and asked me to pass the message on. *All the new young refugees who claimed to qualify for high school should go for the interviews the following Monday.*

Monday came, and we lined up in front of the school administration block. The day was warm and dry, not as sultry as it had been in the preceding December days. This caused the large majority of us—Swazi and *Emashangani* alike—to seek shelter in the nearest parking shade erected for the school head teacher.

Mpaka High School is a public high school where most of the young refugees who still saw school as a stepping stone toward a better life went. It was the closest to the camp and the cheapest for Caritas, which paid our school fees.

After my disappointment at the Salesians of Don Bosco, I understood very well that I had no option but to commute once more. Thinking about that stirred my heart to beat a bit faster. I pondered what kind of life and future lay ahead. A future with no Catholic life. A future with no missionary education. A future with no "quality" education. I was soon to learn that as a student, you created the quality of the education you got—regardless of how rich or poor it was.

While in front of the administration, I learned a little more about some friends from the camp and the Swazis who were present—my potential future classmates. Since our depressing entry into the camp, I had had very little contact with the young Swazis. My very first impression was that they were indeed as complicated as their elders whom I had been exposed to—the police, the camp administrators, and the staff. Their names could testify to this: *Gwebu-xolile*, *Hlop-sile*, and *Celi-colo*—all with uncanny clicks and creepy wording. They sounded weird, funny, or both.

But this revealed another reality too: I was a refugee. I had different names, hence a different label as well. I was susceptible to the discrimination and the stigma that came with all my monikers and my failed attempts to pronounce these clicks and weird sounds. That which I had managed to escape at LIBOSS by pretending to be a Zambian studying in Malawi, there would be no escape from here. The camp was a few meters below the school, and *Emashangani* had been there for as long as God can remember. If I were to be healthy, then I would have to accept who I was. Part of the undesirable elite, the famous yet forgotten beings. And to this description, we could perhaps add "the down in the dumps?"

Interviews, as I came to understand later in life, are usually meetings for liars! And why not practice this important art of life at an early stage? The moment came, and I found myself amid fifteen or more educators. They looked friendly and uninterested. They looked emotionally detached from their interviewee: me.

"Welcome, John Michael." The man whom I soon came to revere as the deputy head teacher of the school kickstarted the conversation. "How are you?" I was still standing, unafraid. This probably puzzled them—my first impression.

"I am fine, sir. Thank you," I responded, my eyes momentarily evading all the other gazes around me.

"So, you are applying for Form 4. Tell us a little about yourself."

"My name is John Michael Koffi," I started, almost as if rehearsed. And indeed, this was rehearsed from the countless interviews we had had with the police, with the Ministry of Home Affairs, with strangers—with anyone, really! "I come from the Democratic Republic of Congo, and I am a refugee here in Swaziland."

"Koffi, when were you last in school?" asked one of the panelists. They formed a semicircle and sat in seemingly comfortable couches. The interviews were taking place in the school library, where I soon found out the staff members also held their meetings. All the bookshelves—three, to be specific—had been pushed away in one corner to provide the needed space. My thoughts flew back to LIBOSS, where there was a large library full of books and learning materials. I thought of the air conditioners, then the computer lab, then my former teachers. All that I had given up by blindly following my family.

"Last June, mum." In Malawi, we addressed female teachers by "mum" or "madam," and I thought it would be the case here in Swaziland too. It worked. Upon me saying "mum," the panelist smiled and looked down at her scrapbook, on which she was probably writing something.

"And where was this?" another unfamiliar face chimed in, dutifully.

"In Likuni Boys Secondary School, situated in Lilongwe, Malawi." By the time I started the word "situated," my voice was breaking. I had convinced myself that Mpaka High School would be a fresh start and hence had no intention of talking about my former life. I finished the sentence with a shaky voice, and my face suddenly shrank from everyone. My eyes retreated and my gaze redirected to the floor, but before I could start *meditating*, another question followed: "What class were you in?" I started to lose track of who asked what! I might have sensed that they were thinking of me as an insecure character, which was clearly demonstrated by the fallback in my composure. I tried to regain my confidence.

"I came after ending my second year of secondary school," I started explaining, and here I found the mendacious art so close and so convenient. I had to perfect it. So, I let that first part sink in while I observed their confused faces. Mr. Petros had taught me well, and I could almost read their minds: *"Second year of secondary school ... Form 4 ... kiddy jokes?"*

In letting that statement percolate, I had time to formulate my next statements using the limited, broken English I had. It had been only three years since I was exposed to the language, and you really did not get to practice the language that much when you were surrounded by five other languages or more. Even if society told you that you must learn English for a better future, and experience told you that you must speak an international language because you were constantly on the run as a refugee—part of the undesirable elite, a famous yet forgotten being—*reality* forces you to speak your local language. It was the only thing that connected you to your culture. Besides, you learned in history about colonization and all the associated nasty stuff that claimed your ancestors and led you to be where you were. Result: those praised foreign languages became less of a priority. That is, if you did choose to be educated. Although again *reality* kicked in and forced you to believe that indeed there was no other way other than adapting to time: time as a constant change and time as a changing constant. In that way English became important, because you needed it for such interviews, needed it to propel you in the journey of life. I had to make myself clearer. As one of the interviewers almost raised a voice to inquire about my tall tales, I resumed:

"I finish the second year of secondary school which is like Form 3 here because there in Malawi primary schools ends in Grade 8 while here they end in Grade 7."

Clarity. Was there sense in these breathlessly uttered words? The following questions were brief and straight-forward. As I was a refugee, they knew asking for documentation would be out of place. They had an obligation to admit the applicant and hope for the best. Just launch the ship and let the current take care of the rest! So long as Caritas kept supplying the school fees and the fees actually found their way out of the pockets of those in charge of the camp and into the school's bank account.

Some of the best students in the school have always been refugees. I promised them my determination to cope with the academic situation. The ability to express myself clearly in English—my peculiar accent and partial vocabulary notwithstanding—indicated my fit for the fourth form, and that wish was granted.

When I learned about this minutes later, I regained my long-lost smile, for at least I was soon to be in an academic setting. Was I being overly enthusiastic? I would ask my best friend Guitar in the following days, who would tell me that indeed, things were what life wanted them to be. I just had to keep plucking the strings and creating the right harmony—within and without.

New Year's Day became my favorite day of the year in this refugee camp. It seemed to spark hope and life in all the youth in this miserable life—all thanks to Imma, who took the initiative to toil in Manzini beforehand so that he could get something to make noise with. The fireworks he bought were an unlimited source of joy to every young one. No one would sleep at night, and if you tried to, you were sure to be awoken at some point in time. All the houses and shelters in the camp had holes for one reason or another, and these holes were large enough to serve as entrances for fireworks that had just caught fire. Whether you liked it or not, the explosive sound of what was sent inside your shelter would wake you up—if not fleeing for your life, screaming that you were dead at last! The memories from the days when bombs and bullets were real would flash, momentarily, but then you would realize that it was just a New Year's Eve simulation from some young adults and toddlers. If you lacked manners, you would accompany the other explosive sounds with a couple of insults before you realized that you were wasting the beautiful voice given you by the Almighty; you might as well join in the countdown as the New Year approached with too much momentum. In this way, the mood of the camp would brighten, New Year's resolutions would be made, those who prayed would pray to their gods, and the whole atmosphere would be filled with both the colorful stench of the fireworks and with *hope*.

But that was only New Year's Eve—and possibly the preceding and following few days.

In January 2013, the drought persisted in the camp, although we were now used to it. I found myself frequenting the now familiar Mpaka High School for water. Every time I found myself in its corridors, I imagined how it would be when I actually was a student. Surrounded by hundreds of peers neatly dressed in the black and white of the uniform that posed a lot of concern to my parents because they were unable to buy it. Whenever we went there to fetch water, I looked at the empty classrooms, wondering which one I would be learning in, which spot would be my favorite, whether I would have a hiding place to escape my unpredictable life, especially since, being a refugee, I was in the spotlight. This thought often sent a thrill into my veins, and I could feel my heart trying hard to pump it out.

The first day of school slowly approached, and I saw life in motion. No notebooks to start with. No school uniforms. No friends apart from my fellow campmates. When I finally made it to school I observed clusters of returning students in black and white—all of whom were siSwati speakers. The grass was brown, and the dust seemed to compete with the sunlight as the wind gave it some energy to move from time to time. You could also spot some flying plastics and papers from time to time, but these were not at all noticeable. The only noticeable thing was a small group of young people, most of whom not in proper uniform, who sat wretchedly at some corner or under a tree having some sad conversations in unknown languages, trying hard not to be seen. *Emashangani!* This went on for quite a while!

I wanted neither to sit with the fellow refugees nor to advertise myself by trying to make friends with Swazis. The more people I saw around me, the more alone I felt. I thought none of them could replace the great friends I had had in Malawi. In Dzaleka, at Umodzi Katubza Full Primary School, at Likuni Boys Secondary School. There was simply none! I was no longer a *Muburundi*, but had become a *Mshangani.* And that ached!

The first day—Tuesday—was a matter of being in the school. The majority of the teachers were not there. The majority of the students were not there. The majority of the day was a waste.

On the second day, out of all the boredom and ceaseless unattended sitting, I started reading *Across the Nightingale Floor,* the first book in the Tales of the Otori trilogy by Lian Hearn. Set in a fictional feudal Japan, the book's plot follows a teenage boy—Tomasu—who comes down from exploring the mountains and finds his whole village massacred and everything burned down. He then embarks on an adventurous journey that takes him through a lot of growth and self-discovery—a mixture of both fate and destiny! I thought I identified with Tomasu, or "Lord Takeo," as he soon became in the novel. Each class period passed with no teachers to introduce themselves and no students to connect with. The next day was the same. Tedium. I read my book. The following day was the same. And I finished the book. I felt well introduced to Mpaka High School!

In the next week, however, the ball started slowly rolling.

"Hi Joy," I greeted a fellow young refugee. She was one of the newest arrivals, a Burundian whom I had enrolled into Form 4 with. They had not yet sorted the classes. How I hoped that we would be in the same class! She looked beautiful and innocent. Polished, with her medium-sized eyes fitting her round face perfectly, her sweet-looking lips reddened by Labello, and her semiblack afro, slightly altered by foreign chemicals, complementing her small height. She was neither fat nor slim, just the perfect size, and she displayed a graceful elegance to look at and fantasize about.

"Hi," she replied. Coldly.

"I remember you from the interviews. We have never talked since," I said, trying to initiate a conversation.

"Yeah. That's true."

"Why did you choose Form 4?" I asked.

"We just came from South Africa. I had completed Grade 9 there," she responded, still uninterestedly.

"Oh. South Africa. School. What kind of school were you in?"

"It was a very nice school. Better than this one." For a while, she looked forlorn and a little bit melancholic. "Although I had to take a train every day to go to school and back," she added, staring at her feet. *Frustration!*

"Train? I have never seen a train," I interjected, somehow embarrassed for disclosing my backwardness, for having not seen a train. But this drew her attention back to me.

"Really?" She seemed shocked.

"Yeah. I have only seen a railroad. There is one around here, if you ever have time to explore it, at Mpaka railway station. Perhaps we can explore together."

"There were no trains back home?" she asked, starting to be a little more cheerful, and sadly, ignoring my latter assertion.

"I don't know. I really never used to travel that much. My parents always said it was dangerous. And I don't remember any, I think there were no trains."

"I guess we have different experiences then, we've all lived in different places." *What did she mean by* all? I wondered inwardly, especially since I wanted everything to be about the two of us. But I picked up on this and asked my next questions.

It was in this conversation that I got to understand the problems that forced her family out of South Africa. I would never have thought of a refugee preferring Swaziland to South Africa, where life is. From boarding the "Transnet Freight Rail" daily while traveling to and from school to sitting in the sorrowful misery of Mpaka and commuting to Mpaka High School; from the rich life to callous poverty, *pakela,* and the Malindza Refugee Camp administration.

I understood the divorce, the husband fleeing from his country of refuge with all his daughters except one—the eldest. The husband fleeing from his wife. The family separated for no apparent reason. At least that was the side of the story that I heard from its teller.

In the camp, the story of Joy and her family that circulated among other refugees was a bit different. Joy and her family were Rwandan spies who came into the camp working for Diaspora, a Rwandan government organization that aimed to track and destabilize all the Hutu refugees and expatriates. The fear about Diaspora was well grounded. But who could tell the specific refugee claimants involved with the organization? Sometimes it was funny to think about!

Most of the Rwandan refugees lived in that wariness and apprehension, wondering how tomorrow might be. As did the Congolese, the Burundians, and the Somalians. They all treated any new refugee coming from somewhere else with suspicion regardless of their country of origin. They isolated many, discriminated against a lot, and forced even more into seclusion. Social life across the communities naturally became unheard of!

This was reflected in the young refugees, too. When parents said to "beware those guys," young people's eyes became wide! Little did any of these loving parents trying to protect their youth from danger understand the seeds they were sowing: the seeds of hatred. Even if the danger had proved to be well founded, they were merely passing on the abhorrence they possessed deep within. But at school we were all forced to be refugees—not necessarily Burundians, Congolese, Rwandans, and Somalians. We were all *Emashangani*!

A million thoughts dominated my little brain as I continued to converse with Joy. At least she had opened up to me, and we had shared some parts of our lives. Did we hide how we truly felt about each other's families after what I had heard about her family? Could I have told her about the other side of the coin that I knew—the unofficial side, at least? Time elapsed!

"So, what are your hobbies?" I asked after getting enough of the disconcerting talk. After all, we had no one else to talk to.

"I like poetry," she replied.

"Me too! I write poems."

"Really? Can we write one poem together, now?"

"Sure, why not?"

"You choose the title!"

"Okay. *Where Do I Belong?*"

After two, three, four weeks into school, I started to get used to everything. The smiles from teachers accommodating my broken English and their enthusiasm whenever they observed my participation in class. The boring, everlasting, forced siSwati lessons. The antipathy and contemptuous looks from some students. The learning experiences and growth. I was starting to get used to the school rules, most of which were obvious, though they had to be constantly enforced through corporal punishment because none of the students cared; Coming late to school, not doing the school homework, making noise in class—the kind of things you would expect in Grades 1 and 2 yet were found in Forms 1 to 5. High school. I was determined to be the exception, but it didn't hinder my English teacher from getting to me.

One good morning, I sat in class with too much composure, even though I had forgotten to submit the homework he had given the previous day in this morning. In fact, I did not forget—I didn't know because he had indicated this crucial detail in siSwati the previous day after he finished his English lesson. He came to class, read out the names of those who were to be beaten, and ... bingo! I was among them. Dumbfounded.

I remember how unwillingly I stretched out my left palm and how his long stick landed three times on my innocent finger joints. I was a victim of the language, and this beating forced me to *meditate*. How I wished I were also learning in my country, a place where I understood what the teacher said even if it were a local language used in a lesson supposedly about a foreign tongue! But how could that be possible? I thought of all the suffering I had endured all my life, the cruelty of people and how they enjoyed that. Those who beat were as good as those who raped, and those who amputated, and those who burned, and those who shot, and all those—my God! They have anger in common, the desire to hurt and to ensure that the hurt is felt as much as they were allowed to. But who allowed it? The lieutenant? The *chef d'etat?* Yes, the state laws, or better, those laws created by the heads of their squads. The Ministry of Education did allow teachers to beat students. The culture supported it, too. *Meditation.*

Corporal punishment was widely accepted in Swazi public schools, like most public schools in many African countries. But sometimes it was simply brutality rather than just the punishment of students. I would watch some teachers force fully grown girls to bend down over a bench and place their hands on the floor: the best position in which they could be thrashed properly. Two strokes, five strokes, even ten strokes—the teacher would count the number of beatings joyfully while the victim would clench up or scream to the best of their ability, helplessly. This scared me, and I observed it with so much agitation each time. Education should not be about traumatizing children, which unfortunately was the case here. Nonetheless it communicated a very important message to me: *You are here to learn. This is your stepping stone. Be serious about your studies.* I hoped this was the teachers' intention.

By mid-February, we had learned enough content to be assessed. This was my opportunity to establish my reputation in the school. It was time to impress my father, who constantly encouraged me to do my best and leave the rest in God's hands. I remember well the moment when I prepared to write my very first test in Mpaka High School—in mathematics—and my thoughts fled to the conversation I had had with my concerned father the night I was refused a place in the Salesians of Don Bosco. When I was so sad and utterly dejected.

"What will you do now?" my father had cheerlessly asked. He knew how much I wanted to be in a missionary school and the role life had continually played in making sure I did not get anywhere with the opportunities I had. He probably felt bad about all the disruption for, as the head of the family, he made all the decisions and the rest of us were just disciples. I had seen him cringe once or twice after making a decision that would affect every family member.

"I don't know," I answered, crestfallen.

"There is no other missionary school. At least not any that we know!"

"I won't go to Form 2! I have completed Form 2! At LIBOSS!"

"We will not have the same conversation as we had in Dzaleka."

"I know, Papa. But whatever happens, I am going to Form 4." I was a little obstinate.

"But this time you have little choice, what will you do?"

"I am going to Mpaka, and I am going to Form 4. All this would not have happened had I remained in LIBOSS. But you did not allow me to." The tone of my voice rose higher, high enough to make my penitent dad back off, because I was getting a little sensitive. Something abnormal.

"I have always believed in you, my son," he mumbled. "You will go to Mpaka, in Form 4, and you will do well."

That was his weapon to silence me with: being on my side, telling me that he believed in me. At the time, I had taken a minute or more of silence to think about all the arguments that arose between parents and their children when neither seemed willing to understand the other. When parents were accused of deviating opportunities that their children would have otherwise got, simply because the former had decided for them. When the parents accused their children of being so troublesome, to the extent that they gave their parents headaches when they complained about their useless needs, wants, and academics. "As if

I went to school myself!" some parents would roar in anger, reminding their kids that even though they had never stepped in school they were still able to raise their children into who they had become. I was grateful my parents were not part of this group.

I promised my father to be the best I could be. By then, I did not even know that Mpaka High School's motto is "Become Your Best." This undertaking, let alone my zeal to catch up with all the content I lost by skipping a grade, forced me to work up a sweat. My social seclusion in school fueled my concentration.

In the very first mathematics test we wrote, I obtained the highest grade of 85 percent. The second highest was a girl who was repeating Form 4 for the third time. I looked at my paper and smiled. The teacher looked at me smiling, and smiled.

School had just started!

One sultry afternoon in March, something happened a few minutes after I came home from school. Things had been happening, as usual. It wasn't uncommon for people from different countries of origin to start insulting each other for no apparent reason. There were always tensions between the Rwandans and Congolese, Burundians and Congolese, Somalians and Burundians, Rwandans and Somalians—I thought it was horribly too much. Sometimes it arose from resources that ought to be shared. Sometimes from news going around about the politics back in their countries. Sometimes from getting too many drinks from outside the camp. It was always outrageous.

Every time there seemed to be some chaos, however, I tried to retreat from the main public. My father had warned me about indecency and my presence around it.

"Even if you don't get directly involved, an element of your brain is affected," he had said. "You don't stop thinking about it …" Every time I thought I understood my father, he would add something else that made me scratch my head; "Stay out, lest you find yourself in investigational follow-ups." And I obeyed. Things that did not concern me directly, I avoided and tried to query later. Besides, watching the same show everyday—how much fun was that?

This time it seemed a little too different. There were noises and screams and shrieks from different corners of our small hellish place—in different languages, too. The Pentecost? I asked myself, trying to remind myself that it had been a while since I even last held a Bible! No wonder things seemed to go wrong day by day.

"Yesu we!!!"

"Murderer"

"Yesu!!!"

"Ahhhh! Yebabawe!"

"Ivi ni nini maisha ametuletea. Tutaendelea ivi mpaka lini!"

"Turapfuye weeeee! Aramwishe nedzanedza!"

I knew something was wrong. I tried to go outside to investigate, but my mum blocked the door, stared at my face, and uttered an emphatic "NO!"

My father looked at me from behind, intently. I saw this when I turned my back to my mum and faced him, his fearsome eyes meeting mine. Perhaps they knew what was going on. What had been happening while we were away at school? I sat down in the ceiling-less house, feeling curious and a little unsettled. What could have happened?

I left the common area and went to my room to play guitar, but my fingers were a bit numb. I couldn't. My thoughts were wandering to the different lands of possibilities. Bad possibilities.

A few minutes later, abnormally, it started raining. Soft, light rainfall. Before I knew it, I found myself in a trance, or rather a memory. My mind flew back to my childhood, to some of the things that fascinated me amid the unstable climate I grew up in, amid the manmade calamities, the unending sorrow—although back then I could have never realized. The sound of the little drip-drop-water droplets from the sky halted by an iron roof—when we still possessed mansions and workers. I was caught unexpectedly.

Back home, in the great lakes, whenever it rained—as it did often—there were many mixed feelings. Parents rejoiced if the cultivating season had just finished, or had some soft, lighthearted lamentations if the rains were early. It always depended on the season. As a kid, I was always seized by this strong sensation that compelled me to dance, overjoyed. Sometimes I ran out of the house straight into the doorway and stood there for minutes or hours, looking at the dripping droplets from the iron roofs that covered our big houses in the compound, looking at the sky hastily turning darker and darker as more water fell like blessings from heaven. Most of the time the rain was accompanied by hailstorms, and the ice blocks made the scene even more surreal.

Then, especially when one or more of my cousins were there, I would run a bit of a race: run into the rain, get wet, collect some ice, put it into my mouth, run back to the house, giggle, laugh, and be happy while my teeth froze to death.

The nature of the falling rain was always unpredictable. Often it happened that the rain was too heavy to dare leaving the house, and that's when I would watch wretchedly, wondering why it had chosen to disappoint me, because I then knew that I would deserve a justified flogging from my mum if I even began to step into the dripping droplets from the roof or the disoriented fine water particles that diverged from the main droplets and found their way into the entrance of the house. Sometimes I was kindly asked to shut the door and go to bed.

"Rain makes you sick." My mother would start, staring at me. I would pretend not to understand because the magical sound made by the collision of the mass of water, the rain drops, with our aged iron roofs, the terrain around, or even the plentiful plants stretching miles and miles from home was strong and strange enough to mask any form of human voice, especially a soft one like my mother's. I would do this especially when it forced me to kindly forsake what I enjoyed.

"Mama!" I would say loudly, still pretending not to have understood.

"Don't go into the raiiiiin. It will make you siiiick..." She would repeat at the top of her voice, possibly switching languages to make her case more appealing to the judge— her, of course. "Yes mama. Did you say something?" Always the same story. At this point, I would then run my race into the rain, *bla bla bla,* come back into the house, and get beaten—my sentence. It never crossed my mind to question why such a loving parent would take the initiative to beat such a happy kid, a child who was exhilarated by the natural world, by a phenomenon that puzzled him so much that he wanted to be up there in heaven, to see where the rain came from, just to know how it would feel to be up above and fall down to earth. (Not like Lucifer, for he seemed to be everywhere).

One day, while travelling with my mother in an old and disintegrating minibus, it happened that the instant we left the bus station it started raining. I was happy. Although the sound made by the upper part of the vehicle did not give me as much great sensation as did the iron roofs at my home, it was kind of a nice feeling. Drip, drop, drip, drop, it went on and on. It was a very light rain. I watched with great pleasure, observed how the water made its way down the window panes of the taxi and slowly drew zigzag shapes depending on the taxi's velocity. And sometimes, to my amusement, the rain drops hit the glass and ran horizontally toward the rear of the car, in the direction of the trees and the houses and the hills that were moving doubly fast towards where we came from. It seemed like some mysterious wind slowly pushed the water globules the instant they stepped on the window pane, and just like a supernatural hand, helped them to draw the horizontal lines they drew. It was beautiful, enchanting.

A few kilometers later, there was no rain. I was greatly disappointed. How on earth could this part of the massive planet not have rain when my absolute and true knowledge told me when the rain falls it is supposed to fall throughout the entire world—on all the surfaces of the earth?

"Mama, mama," I called in a devastated, moving tone.

"What!" She did not seem disillusioned, but I was determined to nag her and question her knowledge in the world, to make me understand why the most delightful phenomena of the journeys I've taken always came to an end. All I needed were explanations. I got to understand that the rain falls only in bits, in small sections of the earth. Heavily or lightly depending on the area and the clouds. And the evapotranspiration of that area—whatever that is. I was told that the world is so big, so enormous, so gigantic that the rain cannot fall over the whole world at the same time. This fueled my desire to travel around the world once I was old enough.

I got to understand that rain made me sick whenever I played in it, because I would feel cold, start shivering, and get malaria. That my grandma always worried when the hail fell, because it destroyed the crops and there would be no sorghum to make the traditional beer that I delighted in. And there would be no seasonal beans to eat along with my *ugali* and *sombe*. That even cassava itself would not grow roots because its leaves were going to be destroyed, with holes in them due to the leaves trying to intercept the hail storm.

I began to understand that my fascination and exhilaration about the rain—a naturally enthralling phenomenon—sometimes made me a bad boy because I did not understand my mother when she called me. Instead of turning to her to hear what she had to say, I ran into the rain like a mad man in his tattered clothes trying to escape that very same equatorial rain.

And I got to understand that I did not truly understand what I thought I had understood. I felt so sad!

Nonetheless, the next rain surprised my goatherd friends and me somewhere in the fields, instantly raining cats and dogs while the goats that we were looking after ran like the wind to their sheds back home. I savored the great mild drops mixed with air. They caressed my body to the extent that I took off my top garment, like the rest of my friends, and I sauntered toward home. The moment my mother's furious, loving eyes met my weak, ecstatic ones as I entered the corridor of the house, I shrank inside myself. We talked about the rain and me, and she gave me a good beating for a couple of times. I entered the house, and there: torrential rains!

Deep in my endless childhood thoughts, I fell asleep. I rarely had these thoughts, being so preoccupied by an endless trauma and the will to survive the "golden" everyday struggles. The tiredness from school might have contributed to my deep slumber. When I woke up, the camp was much calmer than it had ever been. *Tranquility at last*, I thought to myself. I left my corner and went straight to the living room.

We were blessed to have a new section to live in, part of the "White House," following a family who had resettled from the camp to another town called Matsapa. This house was a bit more spacious. Unlike the section we had in Titanic where rooms were separated by plastic sheets and old tattered blankets, there were wooden planks in between different chambers. The floor was also all cemented, and thanks to this family, the house was well preserved. I loved it more. Since my room was the tiniest of them all, I spent most of my time in the living room. There were no doors except the one on the outside, but curtains had been the replacements for the different compartments.

I wearily opened the curtain to enter the living room, and there was one of my good friends coming to see me. And we had a small conversation, which my family over-heard. She had been waiting for me, chatting with my mum.

"Mungu wangu, amemuuwa!"—she started, speaking indistinctly, when I asked if she knew what had been going on. "He fell like a rock. He killed him. The ambulance just took him to Siteki hospital."

I thought she was as confused as anyone could be. *Who killed whom? Did the ambulance take the killer or the killed?* Her heart started racing in her chest the moment I asked, and I felt somehow uneasy, not sure whether I really wanted to know. She seemed to be instantly breathless and taken aback. After regaining her breath, she started narrating the events.

I was surprised that my family knew most of what had been happening. I had been so focused on my school life that I did not even get to know what was going on in the community! I felt betrayed by my family, who wanted me to be focused on my academics and always kept their calm about what took place in the camp.

It had all started quite early in the year. A Congolese refugee called Sebastian arrived from Malawi, claiming he was on his way to South Africa. My parents, among few other families, received him. My father knew him from back in Malawi, because Sebastian used to be a carpenter and had made one of the tables we used to use when we were still in Dzaleka. We quickly integrated him into the family and helped him with some essentials.

A few weeks later Sebastian felt comfortable and decided to ask the camp management for a section in the Titanic. A few weeks later, he fell in love and settled with a Congolese widow who had been living in the camp since God knows when.

The widow, having lived in Swaziland for so long, had adapted to the rhythm of the changing times. She was quite well off compared to other refugees and had recently bought a grocery shop from another divorced Swazi woman who was forced to move out of the camp because her husband had remarried and left her. Once she got together with Sebastian, he became the shop's de facto owner.

Over time, more and more children visited the shop to watch movies, eat sweets and cookies, and drink Fanta. These were mainly girls. Soon enough, Sebastian was accused by some women of raping those children. It started very small, with some people in the refugee community objecting to it and expressing the inaccuracy and unlikeliness of such a thing as "rape" happening. Some said people were jealous because he was a newcomer and had just got life, and some said he was Congolese—since most of the alleged victims were Burundian and Rwandan young girls. All the girls had barely started to blossom.

However, where there is smoke there is fire—regardless of what burns. The camp management was informed, the police investigated, and things escalated. I never got to know the outcome of this investigation!

On this particular afternoon, Joy's father, a Burundian with four daughters, two in their teens and two right before the threshold of puberty, assaulted Sebastian. Or Sebastian assaulted him! It had become public knowledge that the two younger girls in the family were among the nine young girls whom Sebastian had allegedly raped.

From behind, Sebastian hit Joy's father in the nape of the neck with a brick. He collapsed like a cut tree trunk. Everyone, especially Sebastian, was convinced he was dead.

This happened in in the presence of the public, young and old, which triggered emotional bedlam. Sebastian was faster than the police: before sunset, he was out of Swaziland and out of everyone's way, leaving no trace to the concerned parties.

The subsequent days were very remarkable. More tension grew in the camp. Young people barely interacted, especially if they were of different nationalities. Mothers seldom let go of their young ones for fear of poisoning. Men sat their wives in the blankets or planks sheltering them.

I went to school as usual, with a broken heart and soul. It tortured my mind to see the camp so divided. I wondered what role the camp management played, if any, and was reminded that in my young life, my family had all along been surrounded by wolves under sheep skins! It pained me so much to see the youth so divided, none thinking about tomorrow!

This was the pinnacle of the perpetual conflicts in the camp. After all, after a storm comes a calm, and it is in the direst of times that the soothing breeze normally seems to appear and to reappear.

"*Michael weee*, things have changed!" said my mother. I couldn't define her emotional state and intonation, for she seemed to be confused, somewhat nostalgic, melancholic and excited at the same time. I had just dropped down my school bag and quickly stepped in the kitchen to seize a one-liter jug that contained a treasured amount of porridge left for me from the morning *pakela*.

"What's new?" I queried, with a mouthful of solidified *pakela*.

"Come and sit down!"

"Ha! I wonder what happened. I'm really tired—I've had siSwati today, I'm not in the mood for listening to the ominous stories here!"

"Come and sit down," My mother insisted, something rare. On different occasions she might have said right away that I should go and rest and that we would talk later.

"Okay," I said, making myself ready to repose on one of the naked chairs that my father had built with Sebastian before the latter's scandalous exit from Mpaka.

"I don't know what's happening in Dzaleka, but everyone is leaving the camp."

"Oh! It actually has nothing to do with us here?"

"Well, it does. All your friends have left the camp." I thought this was a little too exaggerated. Besides, how did she know *all my friends*?

"What are you talking about? Ma, I'm tired! My brain is not working right now!"

"Well, I saw Remy today with his family! They are here in Mpaka." I had almost halved my jug. And at this information I slowly put it down, offering complete attention to my mother and forgetting my complaints about Siswati lessons.

"What are you talking about?" I asked again, much keener to let her continue and forgetting that this was my previous query.

"We haven't talked to them yet. But I wanted you to be prepared and to know that whatever forced their mother out of Dzaleka was something considerable!"

I just looked at my mother. She was aging—still beautiful though. I thought she was not yet old enough to start engaging in some senseless conversation, like some old people do. I slowly withdrew from the sitting room, went into my room, and sat on my bed. Pondering. How could it be? The presence of Remy meant the presence of Alberto, for Remy was Alberto's elder brother. I wasn't in the mood for miracles! Nonetheless, I experienced one as I left my room and headed to the private room.

I trod on, slowly, because I wanted to release myself. The toilets were quite far from our new house, and I needed to visit the privy urgently. As I neared the other end of Titanic, I saw an image of somebody whom I thought I knew. The pensive figure was of my height, although a little fatter than I, with a slightly more pronounced darker skin and round face. I was quick to recognize him, with all disbelief that the world could ever offer: it was Alberto, seated silently on the stony remains of what used to be a cemented wall that ran parallel to the southern part of Titanic.

I could not resist the force that pulled me as I slowly walked toward him. Like a somnambulist, I left the track I was following and made my way toward him, without making a sound. In utter silence, I sat next to him, breathed in and out three or four times as if I were doing yoga exercises, and when I woke up from my daze, I turned my stiff neck toward his—an exaggerated motion that could have been interpreted as intentional, even though all along I felt like a domesticated animal raised for meat and being coerced by its owner toward the end of its life—and then my eyes met his. We stared at each other like two hilltops that have exchanged perpetual gazes for ages but have never actually met. Then a somber, but more ecstatic and elated smile started to grow on both of our faces, as slowly as life itself.

This day was inherently different from all days I had ever spent in the Kingdom of Swaziland. Not because of Alberto—my twin friend. Not because we were finally together after such a long period of separation. There was much more to that. The presence of Alberto broke open my mind and compelled me to think about life—not just life in general, but the lives of refugees. Even more, I thought about the lives of young refugees. *Many stories to tell in the future*, I whispered to myself, as my memory scan depicted the typical Dzaleka Refugee Camp, the place I had lived until a little less than a year and a half before that day, the Mpaka Refugee Camp, and some of the stories that had touched my heart, soul and spirit—you name it.

The refugee life is not a normal life. What is normal? A refugee is a wanderer: no proper place to live but a long exodus toward life or death. As a refugee, you flee from your country, sometimes with a planned destination, most of the time with none. What happens when you find yourself in a situation where you have to abandon your itinerary? Why plan if the undesirable human traits make you forsake your so-called refuge? Yesterday it was war. Today it's xenophobia and immigration. Tomorrow it will be poor living conditions, a quest for resettlement, an inability to cope with life. Moving from bad to worse, from worse to bad, it's never better. Government, people, resources. Immigration, education, poverty. Fear, hostility, discrimination. No sense of security. Life is simply nonsense!

That place is better than this place. They have jobs and self-reliance. They will give you a place to stay, and soon you will receive citizenship, naturalization. You pay to be smuggled—you pay all of the little money you have, and you borrow much more that you will repay once you have all the benefits of citizenship. You are happy for the journey, the smuggler is happy for the job, immigration officials are happy for their lion's share as they have to provide the documents to let you through the border gates. The documents themselves will look official enough to deceive any traffic police officer, or at least those who are not in contact with the immigration officer. The border patrol recognizes the forgery and will have to be paid some money, not by the smuggler, not by the immigration officer whom they communicate with from time to time, but by you. The last drop of blood is squeezed from your veins, just so that you continue to convince yourself that in the next leg of your journey, life would be better. Luckily, they let you cross the border, and you feel ecstatic; your smuggler is your God. He has planned everything and now you are going to move on—after all, it is only God who can take you to heaven. All you need is to have faith, to keep believing. Whatever they tell you is true, whether it is to board a truck instead of taking a public bus or to spend forever in the semitrailer, enclosed in the cargo space and unable to breathe fresh air. Unless you want to get in trouble with the police, and the immigration, and eventually get deported, you must listen to them, have faith in them. Bear with them, get transported like garbage, so long as you end up being dumped in your intended destination, it's all fine. Have you ever known any saint who went to heaven without trials? Wasn't Jesus himself crucified before he rose to glory? This is your last trial: allowing yourself to be shipped with your family in the dark with no food, no water.

It's just from Dedza border post to Maputo: not far of course! It's just a bit more than two thousand kilometers of holding on, clumped uncomfortably in the back of a truck, as easy as that sounds! After that, entering Swaziland by trespassing the Namaacha–Lomahasha border will be easy. Just cross the fence—as easy as drinking water. You can either climb up and jump in or crawl right below. At some locations, there are wider holes intentionally prepared for you to pass through. And once you manage to do that, you are safe *Eswatini*! How hard can that be? Even if you don't speak the language, be it Portuguese or siSwati, and your smuggler (whom you have paid everything) has to keep as far from you as tens to hundreds of kilometers, you need not to be afraid. Not at all.

And when were you last alone, even just with your family? Or at least with part of your family, because some had been killed, kidnapped, or wounded such that they had not managed to keep pace, so you just left them behind in hope that they could follow. And sometimes they died slowly in sorrow, having no one to hold on to. Was it the rainforests of Congo, when you had to leave behind your six-month-old because he kept on crying, which was unsafe for everyone around you? Or when you had to lie to that eighty-five-year-old that you will come back for her, simply because she was too slow for you and the rest of the family yet you knew what was coming behind you? When was the last time you were alone, walking for miles and miles in the mild fresh cold of four o'clock in the morning, knowing quite well that you had to hurry, because by sunrise you should be out of everyone's way—out of the way of those of a different ethnicity, armed rebels, armed government soldiers, MONUC?

You are on that journey much desired, a quest to find comfort and safety, and either you make it or you don't. Through it all, you step into Swaziland. And miraculously, just like your God—the smuggler—had told you, you get a lift to the police station, straight to the Refugee Camp, or to the Ministry of Home Affairs to declare yourself. You couldn't afford any form of transportation because you had to give all you had to the mighty, just like offertory is integral to churches, and you had waited for more than enough hours for your salvation. Now that you have reached the Swazi officials, you think—wish—it was your time to relax. But no, there would be much more coming your way.

You are physically and mentally exhausted: they go hand in hand. You fill in questionnaires you don't understand, sometimes requiring an interpreter whom you will have to pay in one way or another, sooner or later. You have to answer God knows how many disturbing questions about your personal life, your flight, and all of the past you just wish some powerful Being could erase from your ever-weakening memory. You have to be a good storyteller to formulate how you arrived to where you were without any element of truth. This is just the beginning: they will come for you once you are in the camp. The police have to do some screening, an interrogative process that also lasts forever and often leaves you traumatized, not sure of what you said or who you talked about. The Ministry of Home Affairs has to follow up, and perhaps in two years, five years, or even ten years you will be interviewed for refugee status. All along you have been an asylum seeker, an unrecognized refugee, a person with no identity—and this only means one thing: you are a prisoner of your own making. No official documents, because you are not official anyway. If you are lucky and get the refugee status, it is yours. But not forever. You have to renew it every two years—at least that's the case in Swaziland, but it varies from country to country. They do this so that in case you become trouble they can have a reason to refuse you the renewal. Then you are damned. You know well that you are a curse, so there are no surprises. And if you don't get refugee status in the first place—well, screw you. Wherever you entered, you must exit from there. As the government did not help you in your endeavor to penetrate through the fence (which they intentionally constructed to keep you away), they will not help you to penetrate through for the second time to leave their land. Their peaceful land. All they will require of you is to not to be found on their soil after a specified amount of time. Often between twenty-four and forty-eight hours.

But whether you qualify to be a refugee or not, it will be decided later. Three years, seven years, or more than that.

You just have to sit down and *meditate*. It might be quicker than you think, though rarely. Or never at all.

In the meantime, they will arrange for you to be dumped in the refugee camp, where you expected to find heaven. The smuggler worked hard for you to be there, and it is now time for you to survive. You can't mention to anyone who he is for your own sake, even if he is a government worker or a neighbor in that hellish heaven of yours. It's your little secret. You have to nurture it, to keep it alive, even when you see him every day surviving on the sweat he derived from you, and many more fools like you. This is life.

You were born in the refugee camp. You grew up there, enjoying the delicious taste of its dust and despair. At the age of three, you started speaking a few words. Whenever you heard your mother saying, "Nakupenda mtoto wangu," your neighbor said, "Dore uko gisa." You learned both the languages, more often than not, the exact same wording. "I love you my child. Look how *it looks like*." Two foreign languages, two foreign feelings—one meant to build you up, one meant to destroy you. As a toddler, you ran around the camp and its premises naked. Whenever you met a stranger, he was quick to say, "Chimwana cha ndani ichi? Bwerera kwenu!"—whose horrible child is this? Go back to where you came from. A local language. And even though you found it hard to understand him, his stale stare was kind enough to communicate that it was probably time to turn around, and like a soft breeze, slowly vamoose. Time to go and cry on the lap of your confused mother, unable to explain what had just happened. You couldn't, and you would never understand those words in your entire, possibly shortened, life. They were native to the land; their land did not belong to you.

At the age of seven, you were already in the true mood of a refugee. However your mum or dad tried to give you the appropriate education, it wasn't really hard for you to take "Waswera bwanji," the Chichewa greeting of "How are you?" and transform it into "gaswere nyoko"—a horrible Kinyarwanda insult equivalent to "Fuck your mother." You didn't really care, because nobody else cared. Except that when your mum heard you had insulted someone with such strong, strange words, you were as good as dead—that is, if she were a decent mum. She spanked you and sent you to bring a stick, and beat you so much such that you promised yourself never to insult anyone else in your life. But it happened again tomorrow, and the day after, and the day after that. And during the spanking process, you cried at the top of your voice, cried out your lungs so loudly that none of your neighbors would attempt to go to bed in pursuit of their sleepless, restless night, just because you mixed up the five languages that you were surrounded with, tried to manipulate them into wonderful affronts due to both understanding and misunderstanding, due to the peer influence, due to your environment. If you were lucky enough, your parents were religious. Then, at least, rest assured that you changed to become well mannered the closer you got to your teenage years.

At the age of twelve, you were already in school. Either you were one of the gifted young *Maburundi*, who were very smart in class, or you were one of the typical refugee representatives who had inherited the family's trauma, indecency, and idiocy. It all remained in the DNA, particularly now that you were born in that misery. In short, you were dumb. And nothing could be changed, no matter how many times your teachers beat you, cursed, and often chased you out of class. While in school, you ended up spending more time out of class with friends like you, probably learning how to smoke. And since your parents could neither read or write, you somehow managed to convince them that the red writing on your school report was the best thing you could ever get in school. The school called them for PTA meetings—Parents Teachers Association, whatever that is—and your parents never received the invitation letter. You, the clever kid, managed to get hold of some drunkard or drug seller who was willing to sacrifice a few minutes of his ample time out of the usual drinking, smoking or drug-dealing routine to represent you as a guardian. The school did not really care, simply because they had way too many kids to know who their parents or guardians were. He came and represented you, and you agreed that when the teachers said something negative about you, he would slap you hard and you would run away from school, then your teachers would be very happy because they knew you were set in terms of punishment. Afterward, you would meet somewhere in a dark corner, and you would buy him some *kachasu* or a joint so that you could both laugh at your drama. The money you used was probably that which some good Samaritan offered, if your mum did not sweat and bleed for it. She had kept it in order to buy some tomatoes to eat along with the *nsima*. You stole it, and she knew but she couldn't do anything about it. Especially now that you were a teenager, your voice deepening or your chest coming out, and you felt invincible. Your mother could see that too, but what could she do? If she were a single mother, she would have to hide somewhere under the leaking grass-thatched roof and cry her eyes out. Depression.

It could happen that you were an orphan too. Your parents had died of either heart failure or some depressive disease after you were born in the refugee camp, or you had come along with strangers after your parents had been murdered back in the home country.

Even now, in the refugee camp, you still have those memories. You sit in class, and instead of listening to some nonsensical ideology they try to implant in you, your mind flees to those memories instead, the most beautiful memories. Your dying mother, weeping so hard that you had to cover your ears while watching her spit the last drops of blood out of her lungs. The golden image of your burning father, when a neighbor forcefully held his palm over your mouth, forgetting to cover your eyes, and you observed every unfolding detail of the whole scene of your beloved father being set ablaze while both you and your cruel neighbor were shrouded silently in the banana plantations right next to the open area. Perhaps you were a cute girl. Fair skin, slim body—the epitome of beauty. Eight or nine, right at the age of promising elegance, and you were stripped of your pride. And now that you sit in class in the refugee camp, the only thing you can see in your male teachers is the powerful force of the soldier who entered you so forcefully that you fainted out of confusion and woke up hours later all alone. They had left you, thinking you were dead. As for every female teacher, you just see your mother, or your eldest sister who screamed upon seeing whatever

146

was happening to you, and her voice faded off like a shriek of a night owl heard from a far distance, across a far land where you would have loved to be at that moment. That scream was the last of her that you ever heard!

Better, you are one of the blessed few who have both parents alive. Good for you. Every time you leave school you have to drop your so-called books and prepare *karanga*, the fried groundnuts for sale. You run around the whole camp trying to raise fifty kwacha, enough to keep your family alive for the next few days. The next time you will look at your books is the following day in school, when your teacher asks for the homework he assigned. You will feel so ashamed that you will simply look down at your dilapidated desk. If you were fortunate, you would not be sleeping on empty stomach tonight, because that would make you so weak that in your attempt to hide your eyes from those of the teachers you would instantly fall asleep.

Nonetheless, you persevere. Weeks, months, a term. You are the top of your class.

Time passes and days go by. You are living in the camp, in the misery. That's your home, no matter how hard you try not to think about it. You hear about the beautiful hills and mountains, the lakes, the rivers, and all the natural resources your country has. You see pictures of the Bonobos and the mountain gorillas. You detect a bird flying near you, and you wish you had wings to fly to your motherland. Just for once. Even if you get kidnapped, join the multitudes of child soldiers out there, and get tarnished into a bloody rebel. You wish to see your homeland, which to you is just a mystery. A mysterious playground of some powerful forces of the world.

In any case, all you hear from the adults around you are the sighs of how they wish they were in a position to bring down the oppressive governments. They say they can do all it takes, even if it means befriending the AK-47 shipped all the way from Germany or Russia, or to throw those powerful grenades that the UN peacekeeping mission forces exchange for diamond and coltan. Whenever they talk about this you think of your own dreams. Walking the streets of New York or Adelaide, or stepping in Paris, or some city in Asia where they speak French. Even if it would mean sleeping under the bridge on top of the Seine river, next to the Eiffel tower. You don't even remember where you heard or read of that place—it could be a place you memorized from the recent book you read in your attempt to familiarize yourself with geography. All you know is that you would be safe there.

Sometimes you think of letting yourself let go. Leaving for heaven or hell, resigning from the earthly troubles that have swamped you in your hell on earth—the only alternative. But you've survived all along. You've survived all that. You'll survive all this. Who knows? Maybe tomorrow the government of Australia will offer you and your family a chance at resettlement.

Your mother has already tried to burn down the house and claim that some malicious enemies she doesn't know are responsible. She did it in the middle of the night and evacuated your younger siblings and you. It had worked in the past, and those who were successful were already somewhere overseas. Resettlement. Unfortunately, it couldn't work for your mum, because when the Malawian government realized the trend, they got in the way of any subsequent refugees who attempted to do that. Perhaps all she needed was more creativity. To try and imitate the man who once assaulted his own kids and cut numerous bruises all over their bodies. He wasn't out of his mind! He actually meant well for the kids. If they had received the resettlement to Denmark, it would have been for their own good. He had planned it well with his wife, and the kids were convinced that they should tell no one who the real villain was. They simply had to say that an unknown man dressed in a black mask came and attacked them, uttering insults about their father. The man had said that he would kill him in one way or another. Too bad these kids were just kids, and when given some nice yummy chewing gum and asked what had happened, they emphasized the fact that their father had told them to say that an unknown man came and attacked them at night, uttering bad words and swearing to kill them and their father. And when they were given more sweets and asked why their father had told them to say just that and nothing else, they ended up spilling the beans.

Alberto's presence took me all the way back to Malawi, to Dzaleka. I spent the whole night meditating, unable to sleep for the joy of seeing my friend. Unable to sleep because I wondered whether I would even be able to wake up, and go to school, and waste my time learning siSwati.

Every time I went to school, I came back dejected. I could not get my head around all the things that were happening around me. And now I had regained a best friend, with whom I talked about nothing but the worsening conditions in Dzaleka Refugee Camp. The camp administration there was unable to provide *gaiwa*, the standard mealy flour. Even if they did, the distribution was only once a month, of an amount enough to feed a family for a week. The drought had thwarted the refugees' attempts to cultivate some maize and cabbage in the farms surrounding the camp, reminding the older generation of the refugees the drought of 2000–2001 that hit the whole of Malawi and killed a significant population of the country along with significant number of refugees. There were frequent attacks on the refugee-owned shops in different towns across Malawi, by both the groups of people who were hungry enough and wanted to loot something to eat and those who were simply xenophobic or who became xenophobic upon hearing what was happening to their fellow Malawians in South Africa. The attacks included a few killings of the *Maburundi* that went unrecognized by the Malawian government.

We talked about nothing other than the recurrent harmonious visits of mourning multitudes to *kumuyenzi,* the graveyard which had been secured specifically for those residing in Dzaleka Refugee Camp. We talked of the unending stream of sad stories that had affected him and his family in every way—physically, emotionally, psychologically—and eventually forced them to come to Swaziland. Of course, they followed the wonderful advice of Smuggler the Almighty.

Our conversations were intense and emotional. But somehow, I understood the healing aspect of talking about everything, even though I understood nothing about the psychology of trauma.

And now, seeing the people in Mpaka, the youth so divided, broke my heart. Everyone was living in havoc. Everything was weathering and breaking apart; everything was disheartening and scary.

Mr. Lucky Dlamini was a newly hired camp agriculturist. Or at least he claimed to be: according to the adults he was a spy working for the Royal Swazi Police. He also claimed to visit in the refugee camp for the sake of the youth. It was not by accident that any new worker in the refugee camp would be associated with discordant attributes. A lot of people cared about who was amongst them, but I did not. After all, whether reasonably afraid or not, we were refugees. Away from home you were no one; away from home you had no one. Even if the fear of the unknown got the better of you, weren't you there because you were afraid in the first place? Every time such a conversation arose, many such questions bothered me.

Fear is itself the most fearsome word. Every time you walk you try to force your head into your neck, because anytime the sky might fall on you. Like a chicken at dawn when it is time to get indoors, you open the door slowly, trying to enter silently. You are sure the doorframe is so close to your head that a slight touch would make everything fall on you. The building would collapse on you. A family sits around the table, and the woman is so afraid of snakes that she actually has to remove the tablecloth, assuming they do have both a table and tablecloth, to ensure that there is no snake in between the tabletop and the tablecloth itself.

This last thought always made me smile, for it perfectly described our lives. Fear.

I understood that when you have lived with snakes your entire life, you look at an earthworm and think of a snake. Any suspense is so magnified that there always seems to be a giant ready to seize you, trample on you, and cast you far off, far away from the current present and the uncertain oncoming future.

Lucky looked very friendly and cunning. He seemed humble yet redoubtable. Above all, the first impression I had of him was that of an observant young man, who, even under orders to do evil, would complete his mission having done something good. Isn't that what normally happens in the present world anyway? Take the different volunteer programs organized by western countries. They send people to Africa to come and spy, to find out exactly how to drain the economies of the host countries, but in the meantime build a few schools, orphanages, and hospitals. I had heard this from somewhere. Later in school life I would read and learn about the menacing Multinational Corporations (MNCs), trade unions, and trade agreements whose presence in Africa and other presumably impoverished regions of the world, and their so-called benevolent missions of trying to breach the gap between the wealthy and the poor, increase gender equality, and so on and so forth, only do more harm than good. But still they are given leeway by hopeless African nations. If that happens in the real world, why not in the refugee camp? And indeed, all we need is to adapt to the rhythm of the world and dance to its melody, hoping that the future generations will be better.

I approached Lucky one pleasant afternoon, and we found ourselves talking about the youth in the refugee camp. I expressed my anxiety at the discord. We both harbored the illusion of a refugee camp where every young adult would be as radiant and friendly to everyone as the sun, and where all the youth would be united regardless of the inevitable chaos and quarrels from our beloved guardians and elders. We both envisioned a vibrant, young community where the young people paved a way toward common understanding and the younger generation behaved differently from the experienced and aging. An elusive hope.

We planned an afternoon where we could assemble every single young adult in the camp to communicate this vision. Like a salivating kid whose mother has cooked something special and whose duty was to call every family member in the household to come to the table, I excitedly passed a word to each and every young person whom I came across, and asked them to keep sharing the information. Like a faithful disciple, I was willing to preach until I saw change. I was running up and down, knocking at every door—Burundian, Rwandan, Congolese, Somalian—any door. I was received by the majority. Some nearly slammed the doors in my face upon seeing who I was. *Courage*, my heart kept telling me.

I knew this was my one and only opportunity to bring the youth together as I'd always dreamt. I had a person in a position of authority endorsing the idea, even though from my experience people in such positions should be the last to be trusted. Nonetheless, it was an occasion, a chance to remove the young people from the ongoing conflict, from the hazardous lifestyle we had all assumed. A chance to propagate my "disturbing propaganda" of unity, of progress, of hope.

The afternoon we had agreed on came, and to my disappointment, only few teens appeared. There were more toddlers and juveniles than the teens and young adults I had expected. As much as I liked the enthusiasm and excitement, I wondered what I could do with seven-year-olds, who did not even know the sun rises and sets and certainly did not understand what was happening in the camp.

Lucky was there, and we shared a similar disappointment. Alberto was there too, still getting used to the new life in Mpaka. Together, Alberto and I decided to go different ways and call the peers whom we could find. We started running up and down the camp, once more, like mad men, trying to see who we could get a hold of. We reassembled within five minutes, with a few of our friends. Everyone else had an excuse.

"It's getting late and I have to start cooking," most of the girls said.

"My parents are not there, and I have to take care of my siblings."

"I have to ask my dad first." A more honest justification. After all, seeing a group of teens and toddlers assembled next to the clinic on a quiet afternoon was reason enough to make any of the quarrelsome parents so worried. Even more, seeing them with some weird so-called agriculturist who was known to be working for the government as a spy was such a discomfort. No reasonable parent would allow their children to rub shoulders with that *hyena*.

Lucky addressed us and expressed his wish to see us more united. I was quick to pick up his message and expressed how poignant it was to see people fighting, not fighting the poverty and associated depression that has persistently conquered them—us—as refugees, but rather fighting each other; and to see the young people at the forefront. I expressed my wish to see us working, studying, and spending time together, exchanging more of our ideas and building the camp in a productive way. I talked about the Youth Club shows we would have—an idea that I stole from Dzaleka where different groups of young people could gather multitudes to the communal wall and charge them money to watch them perform different dances, songs, plays, and so on. If God were willing, we would get proper equipment and then start to shine. I could see by the nodding heads that what I said was convincing. Perhaps eloquently said. Lucky himself was caught off guard, possibly because he did not have the slightest idea about what I had up my sleeve once we managed to unite the young people in Mpaka Refugee Camp.

And that was the rebirth of the Youth Club, there and then, this time around as "Swaziland Refugee Youth Association," later to be renamed the "Malindza Refugee Youth Club."

In the previous years, a few courageous young people had tried to build the Youth Club. The most recent had existed for merely a few weeks, three or four years before my arrival. Those who had grown roots in the camp narrated this to me, trying to convince me that forming a new one was a waste of energy. Every time someone came up with the idea of building a youth organization, it died as quickly as it had come into being. Trying to unify a group of young people in a refugee camp you did not own was like trying to swim against the current. If not against the camp administration that turned its back on you, then against the role models—the adults—who did all they could to stop you. I expected this but I did not waver.

My mentality was that I should take the lead and tell the youth what they wanted to hear—the same tactic used by politicians all over the world—and convince them to hold on until we all saw a brighter future, even if that seemed too idealistic. Bringing them together reminded me that while I was in the school library at LIBOSS and at Mpaka High School, I was always fascinated by books that talked about the great emperors and great rulers in the world. These ranged from Sundiata Keita, the founder of the Mali Empire to Shaka Zulu, the Zulu warrior and founder of Zulu kingdom, to Augustus Caesar in the Roman Empire, and more. I did not possess their brutality, nor did I need it. But their courage and their way of convincing those who followed them to spring into action was something I was determined to have. And here, it was just the beginning. I was reminded that in my previous schools I had always led the classmates as the class monitor, and though many had hated me for that, many had loved the order and decency that I brought along with my leadership. I told myself that this was another fantastic opportunity to nurture the leader within me and to fight for what I believed was right and just.

Soon we had our next meeting, where Lucky suggested that we should elect a leading committee of at most five people, who would then decide on the functionality of the club, the meeting times, and activities. They all unanimously pointed at me as the chairperson of the club, without even voting, and then we voted for four more members—the vice chair, secretary, vice secretary, and treasurer. I suggested that we should add another member of the committee who would have no title and who would fill in for other members if they were not available. Swiftly, we drafted a number of ground rules, including when and how frequently we would meet and how we would deal with those who were absent or tardy. Since we had a treasurer and needed some form of fundraising, we decided that if a person was absent they should pay one rand to the treasurer, and if they were late they should donate fifty cents. This never worked!

We agreed to meet for general meetings every Friday evening, starting at 6 p.m. and ending around 8 p.m. I do not recall any meeting where we started or ended on time, but people did attend. Even those who thought the Youth Club was just a joke recognized its seriousness within few weeks and started attending the meetings, although we remained a minority sect compared to the rest of the young people in the camp.

The initial days were all about brainstorming how we wanted the Youth Club to operate, what kind of young people we would like to be, and what our first projects should be. Soon this became a bit tedious, and it was time to really start walking the walk.

We all decided that our camp was dirty, and that we should do something as the youth. The next day I knocked at the camp manager's door asking for cleaning supplies, mainly gloves and large plastic bags in which we could collect all sorts of waste. We started cleaning every Saturday. We would meet on Friday, and decide the time we would gather the next day and what our main focus should be. At this initial step the administration seemed supportive, and the camp manager herself joined one of our cleaning sessions. We would gather all the rubbish, collect it using protective gloves, and burn it. Of course, this produced an acrid stench, but for the next few days the camp would look a bit cleaner. I considered the cleanings a way to instigate a spirit of responsibility in the young people toward ourselves and our community as well as a way to show the refugee community that we could unite and achieve something beneficial for all of us. Later a few daring adults would join us as well, but most of them just observed us and dirtied the camp even more.

Other than unity, my ultimate goal when establishing the Youth Club was to encourage talent development and raise awareness about the many factors that affected us. Soon I introduced a concept of "talent exploration," where we would randomly agree on someone amongst us to present something that they thought of as a talent. This was fun, but it was also exciting to see how people battled their inner timidity and found the confidence to perform for their peers. We did this mostly toward the end of the meetings, after some heated discussions about many different issues affecting the young people of our days—HIV and AIDS, conflict resolution, teen pregnancy and so on.

The meetings became more and more interesting as time went by, and my fear of the Youth Club fading out just like every other that had previously existed started to fade away itself. I would finish the meeting or the cleaning, go straight to my room, and whisper to myself, "Your life has just begun—this Youth Club is your baby and you have to nurture it well." I was inspired and motivated to achieve what many thought was just a waste of time. Motivated that every member seemed to own the club. Even if the number of those who participated and committed to the club itself was smaller in comparison to what I had hoped for, I was tremendously grateful to have people behind me, following my lead, and to have others taking *the* lead. I prayed for wisdom and for God to continue to bless us with stronger ties that would lead us to self-recognition and freedom. I prayed that through the Youth Club one day we could be recognized, that those who sat wretchedly in the camp having finished their secondary school a year or two before I would proceed to university or find work. I saw my friends who had absolutely nothing to do, having finished high school or having dropped out, who loitered around the camp waiting for *pakela* each morning and each afternoon and did not even have a library or a computer lab in which they could waste their minds and time, and I would feel guilty—why was the camp not doing anything? Where was the UNHCR? UNESCO? Did Caritas feel like it was enough to just pay the high school fees and leave it at that, leave those refugees who graduated top of their class just to rot in the Refugee Camp like mice trapped in mice traps? Something was wrong.

We had long known that some people interested in assisting the Refugee Camp residence would get pushed away by the administration. Rarely were the camp residents allowed to interact with any outsiders, especially if they came from anywhere else other than Swaziland. And if they were allowed, it would be under supervised conditions.

We were often visited by the Peace Corps volunteers. They were, as I began to understand, part of a US-based government organization that sends volunteers from the United States to different countries in the world to help in solving critical challenges, promote understanding of United States culture, and at the same time promote understanding of the host country's culture to them. The vice camp manager did not mind accompanying these Peace Corps volunteers (and any other visitors of that nature), who took an endless number of pictures all the way to the plastic sheets and old tattered blankets that adorned the Titanic and separated family spaces. She did not mind walking them all the way to the boys' ghetto, directing them where to go and making sure they saw what she wanted them to see and interacted only with those she allowed them to. This would be done with so much courtesy and overwhelming smiles, but we, the residents, knew what it meant. Soon she would be happy to see the youth cleaning the Refugee Camp, and it would be much easier to show off the camp and demonstrate how much the administration cared about sanitation and the health of its people. But how often did they ever disclose that 90 percent of those who finished high school were still stuck in the camp, trapped in the poverty cycle? When did they ever say that many of that 90 percent were orphans who had nothing and no one and who would love to further their education? Yes, Malindza Reception Centre was small. Quite small compared to larger camps like Dzaleka in Malawi or even Dadaab in Kenya, the world's largest refugee camp. And indeed, the officials used "Malindza Reception Centre" interchangeably with "Mpaka Refugee Camp" to emphasize the fact that it was just a transit point, where refugees would come, declare themselves, and with the assistance of the government establish themselves somewhere in Swaziland. People have perpetually waited for this assistance. They are still waiting.

Life was and is moving there, especially for the youth. I always had this strong feeling of responsibility toward my generation and to find something to lift them—us—out of misery, out of the wretchedness none of us had chosen. I prayed that, united, our voices would be heard. That we would interact with young people in different parts of Swaziland, Africa, and the world. I prayed that we would go far, that we would have a life. I prayed big because I dreamt big.

But the start was rough. There were many ups and downs, many rough surfaces to slide on. We had trivial support from the camp administration and absolutely none from our parents. Everyone regarded us as these crazy fools who were just wasting time. Time. But that was not a problem for me; it was their problem. My only concern was the members of the Youth Club: we had few members, and even those few were not always fully committed. It seemed like some were being pushed into something they did not understand, and they didn't. I, with the support of my committee, had to make sure that we were on the same page with everyone else.

Being the captain, I was determined to sail through the storms and to never let go, to never let my ship sink.

Meanwhile, at school things were getting a little more interesting. The May–June sporting season was getting closer and closer. Per school tradition, Wednesdays were normally dedicated to sporting activities during the season. Students would come to school and go to class in the morning, have lunch, and then participate in various sporting activities. The four major sports were football, volleyball, drum majorettes, and *ummiso*—combined with *sibaqa*, the two main traditional dances in the Kingdom of Swaziland.

I loved the cultural dances. Besides the culture shock which, upon my initial exposure to *Ummiso*, had mocked my eyes as they tended to stray to the upper body of the female dancers who were more than half naked which was something categorically unheard of in my own culture, I delighted in looking at how legs were thrown in the air up and beyond the back of the shoulder and returned down below in an instant. The unified attire was beautiful too. And when all these met the drums beating in unison, they had the capacity to transport a stranger away from the moment, to a trance somewhere in the land of cultural beauty. The males' abdomens seemed constricted, and for them to still be able to raise their legs to their heads was as impressive as scary, but all in all very delightful to watch. How I longed to be able to do that! How I longed to have a cultural identity I could be proud of!

The more I was exposed to these traditional dances, the more I wondered about the seductive nature of the dancers' attire. Could it have anything to do with high rates of HIV/AIDS that has plagued the kingdom since God-knows-when? But I was just wondering. It was very amusing and distracting. And that was, in my perspective, the only authentic form of sports we had at school—training *timvombi nemajaha*, the future Swazi generation who would be able to pass on the tradition as it was, in its purest form. Where did I belong? It always made me question.

Forget drum majorettes dance, which seemed to be a copy-and-paste of some form of creativity imported from Western choreography, even though it had a section called "African dance." The whole idea of an "African dance" on its own seemed very bizarre for me! The Africa that I was starting to appreciate was full of cultural diversity, where in my culture, a young male full of adolescent energy and vigor had to meet trouble halfway, before being able to take a simple glance on the blooming buds of a young female, often betraying his reputation, whereas in the Swazi context you could stare and salivate however much you wanted. This diversity allowed me to differentiate an Ethiopian or Somalian from a Burundian or a Malawian by simply looking at their hair. Additionally, I learned how many of the thousands of diverse African languages intersected: where the peculiarity of Arabic in the far north of Africa fused with some Bantu languages to then diffuse into Swahili in east and central Africa, resulting in the unimaginable beauty of clicks in Setswana and Xhosa. This is not even to mention the thousands of others in between tribal specific languages.

I guess I had issues with anything called "African," although at the same time I admired the efforts to overcome the arbitrary, nonsensical boundaries that divided the Mozambican Chewas from the Malawian ones or the Dlaminis in Swaziland from those in Nelspruit, South Africa. Thanks to the African history I had learned, exploring southern Africa (though by fate) had allowed me to assimilate most of it, and now I was putting the legacy of colonization in context.

African dance was wonderful though! Especially in that most of the time the attached attire seemed to be more preservative and less provocative compared to that in *ummiso*. Forget about football, I had plenty of reasons to despise it! But primarily, I did not want to join because everybody seemed too good for me. Where my own activities were concerned, volleyball seemed to be the best fit. Even with my lame skills, I was still good enough to start recommending to those who were willing to listen about what they should do, in terms of physical exercises that prepared us to play the game. Before I knew it, I was the vice-captain of the team. A huge motivation!

I had already started to have a voice in the school, being at the top of the class in most of my subjects. The teachers were my friends. They saw my zeal to learn, my determination to take in all they taught and then take an extra step to research on my own. Mr. Matsebula, the literature teacher who was in charge of the library and the book store, never refused me any book as long as it was available. Mrs. Mbuli suggested Shakespeare plays that I should read and seemed to enjoy the ensuing arguments with her when I took Shylock's side or denied commiserating with Othello. According to her, *Macbeth* was as easy for me to comprehend and analyze as a simple math equation. Little did she know that I often slept close to midnight, waiting for the late night when using Opera Mini, the mobile internet application, would be cheaper, and then skimming through as many online articles about the prior discussion as possible. I was at least privileged to have a father who had a cell phone and who never hesitated to lend it to me for that late-night research, even though he never knew where he was going to get the five rand for top time. Biology was my strongest subject, thanks to Mrs. Mzumala back in Likuni Boys, who had done everything she could to instill in my friends and me good study habits—and who enforced them through exhausting punishments.

I had proved to my teachers that I was driven, and that reputation was a legacy under construction. Nobody knew my life outside the school. The recurrent trips to Mpaka's public library composed part of a weekly routine. I was hungry for knowledge, and I had to continually prove myself. Not to the teachers, and not to the students. Not to my parents or the on-looking camp administration. I wanted to prove something to myself, because I realized that education was the only way I would get out of the refugee camp, out of the refugee life. A day seldom passed where I didn't hear about people whom I knew in Malawi who had got a World University Scholarship of Canada (WUSC) upon their completion of high school. Then there was Mireille, who had been my inspiration to apply to LIBOSS when I was still in Malawi. She was the Rwandan orphan who had topped the whole country, and the government of Malawi gave a her a scholarship to study in China, as well as Malawian citizenship.

I had met some students from Waterford Kamhlaba (United World College of Southern Africa, UWC SA) and was utterly convinced that UWC was a place for me—just like LIBOSS, I had to work hard to prove to myself that I could achieve my dreams.

My new role as the vice-captain of the school volleyball team was easy. But not to a *MShangani*. Not to a *Ngangawane*—a refugee. Not to a non-siSwati speaker for a team that was predominantly made of bullies. The captain also was a Mozambican whose parents had thought studying in Swaziland would be good for him to learn English and because it was cheaper compared to the English schools in Maputo. The combination of two foreigners leading a school team made it no easier, but my determination was still there. However, the captain had been in the school for the past four years, spoke siSwati fluently, and knew every teammate except the few of us who came from the refugee camp. He came from a rich family too, which raised his status amongst the others. He was a bully as well.

I soon found myself being boxed and cornered within the team. No one respected what I said unless the coach was there. And I loved it! I loved it because it motivated me, although it somehow triggered a form of detestation.

Often when I was tired of playing and interacting with my beloved bullies, I sat down. I sat down and observed the movements in the entire school, but mainly in my volleyball court. I started judging myself because I observed things that others did not. One day I even ended up writing a sonnet, because our literature teacher had just introduced Shakespearean sonnets when she talked about *The Unbroken Chains* as the third book that we would be doing in our literature class, after *Macbeth* and *Amaryllis* by Lucy Dlamini, a Swazi author. I looked at students all around, at teachers who pretended to like their job, at the young refugees in the school cornered somewhere, unwilling to participate in any form of sports because of the level of discrimination which cropped up—however subtle—and then I thought about the flies that I had liked and killed back home. Many of them flying around, others enjoying the human excreta or else licking the human wounds, some of them at my mercy or the mercy of my friends.

"The humans were no more than the houseflies," I thought. And then I stood up, walked straight to the dilapidated backpack I had inherited from one of the refugee students who had recently finished Form 5, took out a small exercise book I had dedicated to poetry, and began writing. The volleyball coach looked at me and smiled. He was also my geography teacher, a job that he hated more than anything in the world. He rarely came to class because nobody monitored the teachers, and always encouraged the students to read for themselves if they wanted to. After all it was their future, not his. "I am a teacher by accident," he confided one day, talking about how his primary purpose in life was to go into geographical research and to be something better in life. Better play around with pH in rocks than spend the whole day looking at the eyes of dumb kids. There were rumors that he was at the forefront of the demonstrations that had happened prior to my family's arrival in Swaziland, where teachers took to the streets asking the government to raise their salaries and schools stopped for a two-month period. He loved volleyball, though! At least for him it entailed some realistic human interactions, unlike wasting one's voice from class to class speaking to young brats who would never make it in life.

He was used to my writing, especially when he realized that the teammates annoyed me. As he smiled, I smiled back. I turned to my poetry book and looked all around to enhance my heartfelt sorrow.

Our life is no more than that of a housefly.

I began feeling disgusted by the human race itself. How was it possible that the hatred and political discrimination that results in exoduses would inhabit even young souls?

This wondrous horrible insect, like us
Lives only the minority of innate hours,
With its existence, by a hair's breadth, a try,

I thought of the deaths I had witnessed and the many more that I would. Time passes so freely, yet human lives are so constricted. Fighting for survival is a natural instinct, they say. But when death came, like a computer-determined algorithm, it was sudden and unexpected, except of course for the few of us whose fate and destiny were intertwined, decided by someone in the high states, sometimes nearby and sometimes across seas and oceans, for those of us who were waiting for death to come from day to day.

Flying but unable to get ahold of the sky,
Eating dirt as it hits upon, every now
and again,
Relaying some ailments devoid of any gain,
With a pair of well-modified compound eyes
But never able to witness what's far away,
And like those filled with disastrous lies
Can hardly have an aim on its only day,
With its wandering life in session
Never can it entail itself in initiation.
We, like it, I wonder the conclusion!

Thanks to the English language that I was now starting to speak fairly well, I could write some simple poetry. First draft, the instant emotions. Editing with the thesaurus to try to sound like Shakespeare himself, I tried hard to preserve my feelings. But regardless of my increasing loss of faith in humanity, I still had *hope*: *hope* that time would take me somewhere, even if time took time to take me somewhere. I still believed in the young people that I saw, clustered in the school like an army of ants with a purpose. I thought of the same volleyball that enhanced my loathing of who I was, of who I have been and who I continue to be, might be the same volleyball that would help me to make great friends and to explore Swaziland.

Indeed, soon the tournaments began. Dramajorates, *ummiso*, football, and volleyball. We went to play to Siteki and to Simunye. To Mhlume and Manzini. To Langa and to Matsapa. For the first time, I had a chance to go out of the refugee camp and its encompassing bubble. I observed with a strong sense of admiration the low-lying lands of Lubombo region. I passed the squatter settlements of Manzini, appreciated the Siphofaneni valleys and delighted in the beautiful infrastructure of Moneni.

I started to get a sense of achievement and belonging. The team was divided at school, but out there we were one, cheering for each other. Even though from time to time my friends from the camp and I were *Emashangani* or *Emangangawani*, travelling for competitions was always special, and it provided motivation to see that there is life outside the camp. There is joy in sports. There might be life after some time!

Schools reopened for the second term, and the sports at school were even more intense than before. I had done exceptionally well during the first term, exceeding everyone's expectations including my own. The boy who had skipped one whole year of academics had pushed himself beyond limitations and obtained the second-best position in class, with an average of 72 percent. It was wonderful! Even if it was not at LIBOSS where I would have gotten prizes, and my mother had no twenty kwacha to give me as a reward, I was very happy that my efforts paid off, and to me, the bar was already set.

In the second term, I would work even harder, aim higher, and never get tired. But I had to balance out a lot of things, as the Youth Club itself seemed already to be taking a considerable part of my time.

When the second term of school started, I had already started negotiations with the camp administration about providing the school-goers with proper facilities for studying. A large hall stood in the middle of the camp and had never been opened to be used by anyone. It had large fluorescent lights that only went on whenever there were meetings or events, all organized by the Ministry of Home Affairs or Caritas. Why not use it?

At first, we asked to hold our Youth Club meetings there, since there was no other place except for sitting outside the clinic, out of everyone's way. We would have our meetings in the evenings. We were granted this, having promised that

I would ensure that the place was always clean and no furniture was moved for any reason. Before I knew it, every single evening a flock of high-school and primary-school learners would occupy the hall. There were only eighteen office-type seats that were placed around a large table in the northern end of the hall, so I had to ask for more study tables from the office. I was stunned when they provided them, and even more shocked that the administration would withhold such useful tools all along, even though they were needed! The refugee housing was very dark, with no appropriate lighting nor fittings to use for learning purposes. We all lived in poverty. Even if we had such accessories, the noise and the heat inside the shared buildings would never allow anyone to concentrate. It was horrible!

The hall on the other hand provided a stark contrast: it was a little secluded from the main residential part of the camp, had many glass windows that could be opened for ventilation, and a very large space that was used for nothing in particular. Having access to it, even if it meant a huge responsibility and risk on my part, made me realize that the Youth Club was a great creation, and that it would allow us to unite and achieve more together. The first and possibly only night I ever felt absolute joy in my heart in Mpaka was the night that we used the hall for studying for the first time. All the kids who did not even care for school, who never studied and just loitered around often insulting whoever crossed their path, were there together with the small few to whom school meant the world. We studied silently, in all the serenity that the world can offer. All the children in the camp were gathered in one place, for the first time! *Hope.*

The twentieth of June, 2013, came quickly. This was International Refugee Day, a day normally organized to raise awareness about refugees in the communities or countries hosting them, and to nudge those who can do something to support the refugee communities around the world in one way or another. It is a day filled with celebration and melancholy: happiness for survival and for being recognized as a person; sadness for being who you are, knowing well that your future is in the hands of God-knows-who; sorrow for the past that you cannot change, the horrendous present, the uncertain future, trauma—mixed feelings! It is a day surrounded by dreams and aspirations, as well as promises that are never fulfilled. By the time it is to be celebrated, there are always embers of hope, but at the end of the day a refugee remains a refugee. Hopeless, helpless, and desperate as usual, especially as this happens to be the day when governmental entities and refugee leaders just show off, pretending to be doing something helpful.

Despite the relative inaction, it is true that in some countries this has sparked true hope—a drop of water to quench the burning throat!

In Mpaka, in 2013, it was celebrated on a Saturday. The Ministry of Home Affairs had heard of the newly formed Youth Club and they wanted us to perform on that day. The camp management had invited some girls from the high school to perform *ummiso*. The girls in the camp joined together and managed to put together some Burundian and Rwandan traditional dances that they would perform as well. Some women in one of the surviving camp's Christian denominations were to sing and dance.

I saw this as an opportunity to introduce ourselves and what we stood for. In the upcoming meetings, we were to dig deep into our minds to find what we could do together, but creativity was an issue. The talent exploration turned out to be much more individualized, and I noticed that this was a gap that we need to fill not just for the refugee day celebration, but also for our own talent development and for the future Youth Club shows. As we continued searching, I remembered one of my favorite songs that we had sung when I was still at LIBOSS, an anthem of the Young Christian Students (YCS), a student-run Christian organization spread widely in Malawian secondary schools. I had fallen in love with its tune but did not know the lyrics except for the chorus, so I had to write my own:

We the youth in Malindza Refugee Camp
We unite to form a group
We call it S.R.Y.A
Because we want it for aye
In refugee life
In refugee life
And everywhere
Let's go together, to change the world
Let's go together, to change the world
With love friendship and unity
Different though, we are one
In colour, in shape and hope
Trying all, to care
To overcome all our despair
In everything
In everything

And everywhere

Little did I know that this song would grow roots and be performed in any public events that the Youth Club was involved in, and would even last longer than my time in Mpaka Refugee Camp—just like my legacy itself.

June and July came with many other exciting journeys too. Whilst the sporting events were going on, there were other competitions in different regions of Swaziland, including the mathematics contest, debate competitions, and the science fair. My school did not participate in the math contest nor the debate competitions, because there was no teacher in the school who was willing to coordinate it—just taking three to five students and guiding them—and the school did not want to contribute the required amount of money for it to enter the competition. Yes, it was a rural school, but sometimes they exaggerated their incapacity! Nonetheless, the science competition took place.

When asked to nominate the school's representatives, the science teachers placed my name first on the list. Sooner than expected, I would find myself at U-Tech, a college and high school that was highly ranked, located in Big Bend, in the southeastern part of Swaziland. Along with five other students, three from the junior classes (Forms 1, 2, and 3) and two from the senior classes (Forms 4 and 5). I missed competing academically!

There were two main sections for both the junior and the senior competitors. The first was the quiz competition, where the competitors answered different scientific questions and whoever answered the most questions correctly was the winner—just like in the old days at UKFPS. The second was the building competition, where each group was given a number of different materials and had to build something that expresses the concept of "perpetual motion." I was placed in this competition with one of my classmates as the representatives of Mpaka High School. I was very excited about this, but very nervous too.

Unfortunately, we lost! Even those who had gone for the quiz did not earn any prizes, and I remember a Form 5 student lamenting how tricky the questions were. He had expected them to be part of the Swaziland General Certificate for Secondary Education (SGCSE) syllabus, the syllabus for both Forms 4 and 5, but apparently most were not. One of the simple questions that frustrated him was, "Why is a red ball red?" whose answer was simply, "because it reflects red light." He wondered where the hell he could have learned this when all the physics teacher at school did was beat the students and speak siSwati all the time in class.

This year was my first in the competition, and I had failed. I was looking forward to the same season the next year, and I vowed to compete again. Though not in the science fair, because even if I represented the school again, this time in Simunye in the northeastern part of Swaziland, I could not make it because we were divided into two pairs and our other pair had cheated, disqualifying our school. We had been asked to build the strongest possible bridge using A4 papers. To test the strength, they put a paper cup on top of the bridge, filled it with marbles one by one until it either collapsed or the marbles filled the whole cup. We had been warned not to attach the bridge to any surface, to make it in such a way that it could be movable, but our friend had used an adhesive tape that held both the paper bridge and the table surface tightly. At first the judges did not notice, but a fellow competitor from a different school blew the whistle on him. We were very angry, because my pair had actually managed to build an even stronger bridge and we were very confident that we would win and advance to the next level, but we could not object to the disqualification.

In this following year, Mr. Simelane, my mathematics teacher, volunteered to coordinate the mathematics competition. Mr. Masondo, my English teacher, led the debate group. Mr. Hlope, the business studies teacher, led the Junior Achievement. I was part of all this, and indeed I did shine in all of them.

For the mathematics contest, four students were chosen to represent the school at the district level, and I was the only one to advance. I competed on the regional level, and obtained the third position region-wide and the seventh position country-wide. I had made it to the top ten in the senior competitors' section, and the next step was to represent all of Swaziland in the Southern Africa competition. For this we worked as a group, competing against other groups who represented many provinces in South Africa, Uganda, Botswana, Lesotho, and few other countries. We did not win, but the country-wide recognition was enough for me. It was that inner voice telling me, "You see how easy it is? You can make it even farther!"

Being part of the team that represented the kingdom of Swaziland in an international competition as a refugee meant the world to me. It made me realize that no matter how many limitations, boundaries, and cages lay along my path to keep me a prisoner of my identity, there would be a way out. One way or another, there would be a way. Perhaps education was that way. Not only education, but hard work and determination, consistency and drive, all in absolute humility. This is the time when my father's voice came to me, and his words made much more sense than ever:

"Focus on your studies. Trust God and your heart. That's the least you can do."

The awards ceremony for our participation in the math contest and representation of Swaziland internationally would be on my birthday, the first of November. I had to go to the University of Swaziland where the ceremony took place. It would be my very first time stepping onto a university campus, and having completed high school by then, I took this to be a sign that greater things were coming my way. It was the impetus for *hope*.

Through all the busy academics and the sporting season, I often came home late and tired. I started to spend less and less time with my friends in the camp, especially those who were not attending school. I only saw them during the Youth Club meetings and activities, and since they did not go to school, they were rarely present in the study hall. I felt bad that I did not interact with some as much as I wanted, for they were my motivation and according to some, I was their solace. This did not hinder me from running up and down in some evenings, sometimes tracking them down where they were being hypnotized by either South African soapies—the likes of *Mvango* and

Generations, or Latin American drama series. A channel called Telemundo happened to be every teen adult's favorite because of the Romantic series it showed, and any one of us who was privileged to have a TV set had a full house all the time! Worse, these things ran twenty-four hours a day. I detested such an addictive form of entertainment. I knew that as much as it served as a distraction from the constant sorrow and distress that was abundantly offered by the refugee life, it was also the best way to waste time! Why didn't they read?

Waterford Kamhlaba's Mpaka community service, in collaboration with two Peace Corps volunteers who lived in Mpaka and volunteered a lot in the refugee camp, had put together a small library. I had hoped that this would be a more constructive waste of time for my friends than movies and television shows. Did I judge them? Probably not. Life can be misleading, especially when you were your own child. Some of them were orphans. Some had been deserted by their parents. For the others, their parents never took time to notice their existence. It pained me to see that fewer had interest in books, and the less time I spent with them, the more afraid I was that they would completely lose themselves. And indeed, some took up to drugs, regardless of this being a topic in the Youth Club meetings. Pornography was there, and for a few, sex became recreation. Minds were being constantly corrupted, and I would dejectedly hear the stories, incapable of reacting, or at least promoting a positive change. My youth, my people! For some reason, I felt like I had a responsibility to everyone, but life overpowered me. And not only me, but also the inner beauty of many.

The majority of those who lived in Mpaka Refugee Camp did not have any official documents. Documents were among those things that we refugees are entitled to but that the established system takes an eternity to provide, and then provides only if you were one of the lucky few. This makes it incredibly hard for the young and the old to access any social amenities, and for qualified adults to find work so they can provide for their young ones.

While at school, and being in Form 4, we had to start registering for the final, national examination that we would have the next year. This required a Personal Identification Number (PIN) provided by the government, and for any other refugee student who has ever had to go through this process, it was an impasse! The school knew this, and on my part and that of the others, we encouraged them to communicate directly with the camp management, but they insisted on sending us back to the camp if we did not provide the PIN number within the given period. I therefore had to visit the camp management myself and ... face the music.

Letters were exchanged between the school and the parents—in other words between the school and me—and phone calls were made from the camp to Home Affairs in Mbabane. There seemed to be a way, possibly because the camp manager was very supportive when it came to me and my family. I had earned this, through my first days in the camp working when and where no one else could, through my industry at school, and now the Youth Club. They had no reason whatsoever to deny me what I deserved, even despite the inevitable complications. At last I went to Mbabane, carrying tons of letters from the school, the parents, and the camp management to convince those who should be convinced why I had to get a PIN: I would sit for SGCSE next year, and registration started now.

On Monday the fifteenth of July, I got the PIN after many actors had played their part. This day was a huge leap forward not only because of the PIN but also because of the new robes I would soon wear.

While I was away in Mbabane experiencing these twists and turns, the assembly of teachers convened in the library. There was no school the whole day, so I did not miss much! This was the day when they would elect a new team of prefects to replace the old ones as the students in Forms 3 and 5 were soon to start their national examination. The class teachers went to their classes and asked the students to nominate those who they felt would lead them. I heard that none of my classmates nominated me! The teachers went on to call individual students whom they thought would be good prefects, interviewed them and discussed them after the short interview. I had no idea that this was taking place, especially on my day of absence. But the next day would shock me.

During my time at Mpaka High, the school assembly was held every day of the week. I had cynically laughed at this waste of time. Why not use the thirty minutes for a morning study session and assemble just once or twice a week? The next Tuesday, the deputy head teacher had to announce the new names of the prefects, calling them in front of the whole student board. The teachers normally chose prefects from Form 1 to Form 4, so that in the following academic year, every class other than form one would have prefect representatives. The stereotypical prefect would be impressive in class and reputable outside of class. In the 2013 academic year there were thirty-two prefects, but for the 2014 academic year they wanted half the number. Six would be the leading prefects, including the Head Boy, Head Girl, and two vices for each. Then ten others would be class prefects to assist the leading six.

They called the names in order from Form 1 to Form 4. I observed the shy smiles of those who were called, as the entire school burst into applause as if it were an inauguration of some kind. It was great! Second Vice Head Girl; Vice Head Girl. Second Vice Head Boy; Vice Head Boy. By this time, I was wondering why on earth nobody had nominated me, and instead of clapping for the others, I was caught up in my own thoughts. I had thought of what I would change in school had I been placed in a leadership position.

The Head Girl—Ziyanda Simelane, was a classmate of mine. She had an amazing voice, the most angelic I'd ever heard, and she always led the morning singing on assemblies. Her reputation was indisputably worthy of the position.

The Head Boy—John Michael Koffi. I stood in my shoes, feeling a million tiny little insects climbing from my toes to the tallest of my thin hair. I had thought no one nominated me, so I had assumed I wasn't under consideration. I was wrong. Having been away the previous day, this unfolded like a dream or a vision. My name was called, probably at the wrong time, for I was caught so unexpectedly. How could it be? I had stood in front of the whole school only very few times, either giving motivational words, presenting how our volleyball team had done in the tournament or being recognized for an achievement of some sort. And for all those times I had somehow managed to rehearse what to say, and how to position myself in front of everyone else. My legs became stagnant, for the shock of having been selected to be the Head Boy of this school, as well as the awkwardness of being caught off guard.

"*John-Michael-Koffi*? *Ngim'bonile*, is he here?" The deputy called once more, mixing his siSwati with English as usual, indicating that he had seen me and asking if I was there. And there I was! I was getting back into my senses, hearing the cheers and applause that came from every corner. The classmates in front of me made an opening, and slowly I made my way to the stage. A young *MShangani* the Head Boy of the school. The chairperson of the Youth Club, the Head Boy of Mpaka high school. Who saw this coming?

From the outset, my school life changed. A mixture of joy and fear seized me, and every time I walked I felt as if I was staggering. I could look to my left, to my right, and turn my head slightly to see behind me—the eyes on me were uncountable, and they conveyed different messages. Then I could look ahead of me, stare at the ground in front and walk on. I avoided as much eye contact as I could, and from time to time I felt embarrassed just to walk in the school premises. "Ey, Head-boy?" A student could call from a distance, just for the fun of it, and I responded with a combination of a smile and glance that lasted for a few milliseconds. Many spoke siSwati to me, knowing I did not understand a single word of what they said. But then the chuckles and cynical screams that followed would point me in the direction of their amusement, telling me that

I had been teased or bullied. Others came with enormous grins and bowed in front of me, saying "Greetings my Head Boy." Their friendliness could be reciprocated in one way or another. In class I sat uneasily, burying myself into my books once more, but the few friends I had couldn't help but come to talk to me about the new shoes I was wearing.

News traveled. My new leadership position reached the refugee camp before me. The moment I stepped in there, everyone was also looking at me. A couple of "congratulations" coming from the heart were there, but I sensed some grinding teeth as well. My parents did not know how to react. Even now, I still wonder what they thought of the news; they hardly expressed how they felt about the unfolding of events.

That night I slept in an unexplainable mood. I was happy that I gotten the leadership position that I craved, because I wanted to see so much change in the school. I was a little anxious because nobody had even asked me whether it was something I wanted or prepared me to play the role effectively! But I knew deep inside that this was by no means a mistake, and that it would all go according to the meticulous design of time. I slept well!

Sugabo, Alberto, and I had been practicing for a while, preparing for the Youth Club performance to showcase our talents and bring together the community. We were far from perfect, but we were prepared to do our best. The three of us drew inspiration from the performances we had seen back in Dzaleka, having all lived there.

"My man, how prepared are you?" I asked Alberto, trying to get a sense of his readiness. He seemed to be disconcerted and I wanted to bring him back to reality.

I still possessed the dilapidated phone I had bought from James while still at LIBOSS. I had formatted its memory to be able to add three different instrumentals of the songs we hoped to perform. "You're not fully concentrating—this is the second time I've played the instrumental." I added, looking straight in his eyes. Sugabo was the quiet one who always waited to be told what to do.

"Sorry *wangu!*" He replied. "Play it again, *ayise.*"

I played the instrumental, and then he asked me to pause. At this point, Sugabo thought it wise to leave us alone because he probably knew there was going to be some deep conversation or a lecture. He was used to the two of us. He was a Rwandan of about my age, reserved and observant.

"Michael," Alberto started, somewhat coldly. "Do you remember the time we used to sing in Dominiko Savio?" he asked, and I replied a simple, but somewhat perplexed, "Yes."

"Do you remember the times when we used to go to church every Tuesday, Saturday, and Sunday—just for the sake of singing and praising God?"

"Yes, I do."

"Here we are now." A long pause. A long sigh. Awkwardness. "Why don't we have church here?"

"Because we are in Swaziland, and not in Malawi. Because this is Mpaka Refugee Camp with a few hundreds of refugees as compared to the thousands in Dzaleka, and with very few Catholics who cannot put any shit together to build a church. Do you want me to go on?" I asked, a little bit peeved, and quickly realized that I was crossing a boundary. Then I lowered my voice, "Plus, we do meet on Sundays and ..."

"Sometimes."

"Yeah, and ..."

"Only your family, Phindiri (the camp manager) and I."

"But why are you suddenly bringing this up. What are you trying to tell me, Alberto?"

A long pause. A long sigh. Awkwardness. All our preparation for the show seemed useless for an instant. Invalid.

When I first dreamt of the Youth Club, I had imagined the amazing performances we would put on and how we would invite all the refugees to participate as the audience, to be entertained and momentarily forget their toils and troubles. We hoped to smuggle in the camp officials too, and perhaps some workers from the Ministry of Home Affairs. Either way, I dreamt big. This was my first attempt to bring this dream to life, and the youth were indeed engaged.

Sugabo was coordinating a Kwaito and hip-hop dancing group. Joy was overseeing all those who planned to do the singing, and her sister, Keza, was leading the Burundian-Rwandan traditional dancing group. A few others prepared poetry and some were just followers, ready to take on whatever was asked of them. Zoph and Dirick, a charming, wise Somalian guy, were the ones communicating with the outside world, trying to make sure that we had the loud speakers and microphones, the amplifier, the decorations and other few materials we needed for the function to go well but rarely got. They were the oldest and had joined in the prior attempts to build a Youth Club. When Dirick got to hear about my initiative, he was quick to investigate his memory and his piles of papers to see if he still had the constitution that was once drafted for the club they had formed before. He helped us name it the Swaziland Refugee Youth Association. I was directing a short play and overseeing everything. We had support from many more young people, even those who were not members of the club, and it made me happy. Alberto had declined to have any particular role, but he supported me in each and every way.

Sugabo, Alberto and I were practicing two songs: "My Love" and "Queen of My Heart," both by Westlife. It was a busy time for everyone, especially for me, and I hated to see Alberto's absentmindedness. However, it is in such times that we learned a lot about each other, and appreciated the lives we had—or not.

Alberto and I had been raised to believe in God and to serve God. Living with no choir, no altar boys, and no mass to attend seemed to affect us more than anything. But I understood that there was much more than religion and spirituality. After all, when you can trust no one around you, even your peers, and there is nothing to bring people together in the community from time to time, to share ideas and ideals, to share beliefs and culture, to unite, who do you turn to? For Alberto, this matrix was also complemented by the fact that his parents did not pay any attention to him, did not understand or help him to grow as a young person. He had been always influenced by the people around him, so he needed a strong community. Mpaka Refugee Camp lacked this! The Youth Club was there, in action, but wasn't it the very same Youth Club whose supposedly mature members cursed and confronted each other in front of their nearest and the dearest?

There were followers of the Roman Catholic Church in the camp, but none committed to coming to a church service that was seldom delivered there, other than just two families, Alberto, and the camp manager. There were other Pentecostal denominations too, one of which had disputed and separated into two. There was a minority Muslim community, mainly dominated by the existing Somalians. The majority of the camp residents were dormant Christians, those who had already given up on God.

In a place where the only hope comes from faith, and everything else seems to be associated with discomfort, rejection, and dejection, people were constantly lost. My best friend was slowly giving up too, but I reminded him who we were.

"Alberto?" I called him, calmly. I tapped his shoulder gently and started my usual preaching. "We are in a different situation here. In a difficult situation. And once you get to understand this situation, we only have to adapt to it."

"Michael, this is hell!" he exclaimed, trying hard to push the trapped air out of his lungs. At that instant, I realized how sad he was. "This is hell, we are only singing for the devil! We will go in front of all these wicked people and sing 'My love,' pretending to be Westlife, then what?"

"Don't you think it is ..."

"I think the moment they step out of the hall they will continue to insult each other, and no one will ever even remember that we wasted all our energy preparing a show for them, wasted resources we do not have, and simply ..."

"Alberto, how about ..."

"How about what? Tell you what, *mwanangu*, I know we are the youth, and as you make it clear in the meetings we will have a better future, which we must create for ourselves, but I'm tired of living in this hell! *Nimechoka mwanangu!*"

I watched his thorax rise, and then his lungs sink in his abdomen, as he gasped some air and exhaled profoundly. For the next few minutes we sat in silence, as if commemorating the dead ones. And indeed, we were dying slowly and had no one to commemorate us except ourselves. Alberto always managed to make me feel how helpless we were, and how the place we lived in was as good as "hell."

But every time I looked at the young people, I saw *hope*. I saw an infallible future, rising from the misery like smoke would appear in a clear blue sky. I saw energy, capable of dying in the outer world but able to survive deep inside if it can hold on life for a bit longer, and hold tightly on the slim *hope* that we had. I saw beautiful souls who would go far given the opportunity. I saw talented young stars who were simply stuck because there was no alternative, but who would be warriors if they realized their inner strength and the zeal to create an empire from deep within. I realized that indeed we were being buried, buried into graves of uncertainty for the future, into graveyards carefully planned by the benefactors of our miserable situation. But no matter how deep they would directly or indirectly bury us, they would soon realize that we were fruitful seeds. These thoughts, unlike my constant meditation, motivated me beyond words. They gave me strength to carry on, to be the captain of the youth while the ship sailed unknown lands. I had *hope*.

The Youth Club Show was announced. It was held on the weekend before the third term of the school started, followed by a party in which only young people were invited. We ate and drank soft drinks, and then we danced, all of us together. No Congolese were there, no Rwandans, no Burundians, no Somalians, or any other nationality that existed in the camp. Even the few children of the camp officials who were there were not Swazis. We were simply young people having fun.

For the first time in my life I felt a true sense of achievement. The camp atmosphere was changed.

The ensuing days became more livable. The Youth Club Show changed a lot of things, such that social life started to be a habit.

One afternoon when many of us sat near the tanks fetching water, we engaged in different conversations. We narrated the stories of how we felt, acting and reacting to our own acts in the Youth Show, messing up the lyrics in our attempts to entertain, but more important, dancing in each other's company. Apparently, there had been some booze that I was not aware of, but that was not an issue. We made fun of how we all looked sharp, and teased those who had tried to latch onto their dancing partners. Great conversations.

At the end, I found out that that Keza was cooking chapati, a form of flatbread very common in East Africa. I challenged her to feed me for the first time. She was one of those girls who caused a light tingling sensation all over my body whenever we interacted. She was a beautiful singer and a more talented dancer than I had ever encountered. She danced mostly traditional Burundian dances, and her angelic shape moved gracefully with the flow, whether to Bollywood or any other type of music. I had never really told her how I felt about her. How I felt about our interlocking eyes from time to time, or whenever I secretly stared at her fairly dark skin which hid any perfect imperfections, and distracted me so much such that I couldn't help but notice her elegance in my own way. She agreed to the challenge and promised to bring me the food at home.

For the first time she dared to come to my house, with a plate full of chapati. The timing was unfortunate, because I was sitting with my father watching TV—a man who scared her to death! She had constantly explained to me how my father was the nicest person she ever encountered, but she was always afraid of him. His presence made our interaction brief and precise.

"Hey Michael."

"Hey, what's up?"

"I'm delivering your package. I'm sorry if it doesn't seem as good as you might have expected."

"Ha ha ha, like any other best cook, you always say that! Thanks—I'm excited."

"See you later."

"Not so fast … eh, okay! Later."

The moment she stepped outside the house, my father gave me this weird look that he had never given me. I didn't admit overtly that I understood what it meant, but I instantly realized what it was. *She is Burundian. Her father is dubious.*

"What is that?" He hurriedly asked, looking at both me and the plate interchangeably, instantaneously.

"It's chapati. She cooked it, and I asked her to bring me some once she finished. That's all!"

"You are not eating that. Are you?"

"Why not?"

"Michael, you are not eating that! What if …" He hesitated. I looked at him, and then I left the living room. I wasn't used to judging my own father, for he was the perfect model to my own character. I didn't want the disbelief to shadow my own judgement. I carefully deposited the plate in my room, grabbed one chapati, and went off to see Alberto and our other friend, Ibrahim, at the far end of the camp.

As I neared their ghetto, I slowed down to observe the magnificent view of the sunset that was appearing over the horizon. Breathtaking as it was, my attention was quickly caught by the conversation that was happening inside their room. Alberto and Ibrahim were louder than normal. Their voices were agitated. I sensed some anger and confrontation boiling, and I hesitated to open the door.

"*Mwanangu*, …" came Ibrahim's soft voice, high pitched than normal. "… what are we eating tonight?"

"I thought you had cooked something?!" Alberto answered hastily, using the same intonation.

"I have flour. *Ugali* would be possible but there is no water."

"Wait, what? I thought the camp did provide water today!"

"There is no water here! *Kwani*, don't you know that there was fighting. Don't blame me for anything my friend,

I didn't want us to sleep on an empty stomach. I didn't want to get involved! They closed the tank when Kikongo started arguing with Apo—." His voice fell. It might be that something distracted him. Kikongo was a Congolese lady well known for her verbal violence. She never missed an opportunity to insult anyone, be it a three-year-old toddler or the camp manager. Her counterpart was a Rwandan who was famous for beating his wife. He and his wife fought almost every single day. Kikongo and her counterpart were the main actors in the camp dramas, and as usual, on this particular day, their play ended with a couple of people not getting water.

"You see, man, this is ridiculous!" Alberto said, a little angrier. He had spent the whole day in Manzini working with some refugees who sold second-hand clothes in the market, who would in return give him a little money to buy flour and oil. "How do you expect us to survive? Yesterday you slept while they were giving water, and you woke up when they closed. Today you didn't even try. *Unafikili tutaishi Maisha gani mwanangu?*"

"It's not my fault. Yesterday I slept because I was stressed."

"It's not your fault? Stop the crap and the laziness man."

"How do we survive?"

"How do we survive? You even have the guts to ask! How do we survive?"

"Alberto, look …"

They continued to quarrel, but my attention was immediately captured by some cattle that had broken into the fence around the refugees' vegetable gardens. I was still contemplating whether I should run and chase them away, when I realized another very young boy was running toward them at top speed. I looked at the boy and was reminded of all the useless attempts my family had made to cultivate maize and eggplants. We had acquired large gardens (like we did in Malawi) thanks to the camp administration, and as a family we worked together to prepare the land and sow the seeds. Everything grew happily and healthily until the loose cattle grazed in the fields, leaving absolutely nothing. It happened five times before the camp officials stepped in. The owner of the cattle was called to the office and they asked my father to name the compensation for all the crops destroyed, but he declined. "Swaziland has given me refuge. When I came here, I had nothing. I wanted peace and education for my children, and even though not all of them have appreciated this opportunity, we have been well received." Everyone involved in the case was bewildered by this response, and they stressed on the fact that something needed to be done—a punishment for all these careless farmers. "Traditionally speaking, all the cattle belong to the King, hence they are free to graze the King's land wherever and whenever," the camp manager had asserted, "but their owners have to be respectful to the crop farmers, especially the refugees who do not share similar beliefs and have very limited economic means to live with." "Well," said my father, seizing the floor once more, "all I ask is that this man and his aides come and help me next week to build a fence around the fields. At least that will solve both our problems without someone having to pay compensation for destroying crops in his own land." Obstinacy flows in our family blood, and at this my father gave the man the date and time, and he stood up and left the room. The man did not have to pay a single cent! The day came and they built the fence. Unfortunately, it was too late. All the grazing had left the crops stunted, and the 2013 drought quickly followed. We never harvested anything!

This flashback took place while I looked motionlessly at the boy chasing the cows. Diamond Plutnumz's "Kamwabie" was playing in the background, from Ibrahim and Alberto's room, concealing their ongoing angry conversation. And suddenly it was not playing. My attention returned to them. I had never heard the two of them arguing in this fashion. I became a little bit scared! I knocked, and they were startled when I opened the door. I invited them to come at my place to watch a Hindi movie, as we called the Bollywood movies, and they relaxed.

As we stepped out of their room, the sun had just set over the horizon.

November 2013 began with some drama, an augur of what would happen a year later. As soon as the second week kicked in, one of the houses was burned to ashes. A Rwandan-Burundian family of six was sleeping in. Luckily, none of the family members was hurt, although they couldn't retrieve even their underpants, let alone a single coin. A lot of water was wasted (amid the scarcity and drought) trying to put out the fire, but all the efforts were in vain. Long after the attempts to put out the raging fire had failed and nature had taken its course, and just when the last flames were dying out as the gathered refugees pathetically looked at both the concrete remains of the house and the distressed family, the fire truck arrived in the camp along with the police and the ambulance. We laughed. The causes of the fire remain mysterious.

Just a day after this mysterious fire which consumed everything but took no one with it, a Congolese child died—again mysteriously! Her mother's reaction was to arrange a way of being smuggled to Maputo. She convinced herself that whoever was responsible should not see the burial, lest the young boy not end up in heaven. It was all heartbreaking. But of course, being refugees, we lived in our dreams for peace and security.

The third school term ended. Another learning opportunity presented itself.

Apparently, the ministry of home affairs was very thoughtful about the well-being of the refugees, and they initiated a building project. Two brand new pit latrines were to be constructed, to be shared by over three hundred refugees, young and old, along with the two other latrines and a receptor tank that had to be dug, all of which meant that more waste would be produced. I never really understood the logic, but thanks to them, at least a few of us had something to be kept busy with over the school holidays.

The curious minds of the refugee camp were made to believe that within the coming months and years the human waste sustained in the receptor tank would be emptied and then used as fertilizer in the farms belonging to refugees. I found the idea quite amusing, having taken agriculture as a subject in my last years of primary school and first part of high school. I wondered how long it would take for all of us to produce enough shit to be shared in all the refugee farms that had been struck by drought. But even more amusing was the fact that the receptor, just like the pit latrines, was right in the middle of the camp! A little far from official eyes, but near enough for the refugee settlements. I imagined the smell, let alone the living things it would attract. This made me think of the families who often tried to escape the heat and the noise in the Titanic and sit outside, cook outside or even socialize outside. I imagined the toddlers who were always running around, naked in their innocence, then I closed my eyes and hoped that the receptor tank would be concrete sealed, and that the pit latrines would somehow be closable. But these were all my imaginations, so I kept them to myself, zipped my mouth like nothing ever happened.

Babe Dlamini, a Swazi builder who had been hired to work on the construction invited a number of young people to work with him, promising a great deal of money. The camp administration insisted that we should help, since we would be paid to build what was important for us.

As experience is the best teacher, we were always wary about the swindling that had become an integral part of our lives. Lies about payments were so common that all the youth, especially the members of the Youth Club who were well accustomed to them, decided to pull out once and for all. Many thought back to a few months earlier, when there was a biogas construction project in which all the refugees who participated did so out of a strong sense of commitment and fulfillment for having done something out of the usual boring life of a sloth, but of course their pockets were full of nothing but deception. The biogas project had been an initiative of a Waterford Kamhlaba refugee alumnus who wanted to do something good for the refugee camp that had shaped him. As a volunteer I had participated wholeheartedly, with a slight envy for those who were promised money! My reward was beautiful talks as we dug the dome-shaped craters which would be the base of a mixture of human wastes, cow dung, and whatever it took to create the biogas. One conversation sticks to my mind especially, when one of the camp elders, Papa Musa, asked me whether I was hoping to go abroad on a scholarship and I answered that I was. Being a little more knowledgeable, he quickly asked me about brain drain and personal transformation, and I hastily vocalized my wish to live in Africa, no matter where I went. He knew of the despair that existed and played that card to convince me that out of all the misery and desolation; if I were to get a scholarship I would do whatever it takes to remain in the West, and accordingly, I would transform into a different person due to the liberalism prevalent in Western countries.

"Suppose your sponsor is gay," he had said.

"Gay?" I answered, a little flabbergasted since that is not something I had ever talked about with anyone. Even my father!

"Yes, gay." He resumed. "Your culture does not accept, does not tolerate the use of a condom, let alone homosexuality."

"Condom? Homosexuality?" I found myself repeating after him, like a confused parrot. I felt a little uncomfortable, having such an embarrassing conversation with a devout Muslim who was possibly more than forty years older than me. But he looked friendly, and he seemed to have a message he wanted to pass across. After all, throughout the strife in

Mpaka, I had unknowingly convinced those who observed me with my strong persona with an open-minded world view. I was told after this conversation!

"If your sponsor is gay, you will spend your first year of study trying to figure out who you are. Then you will be brainwashed and be made to believe that you are what you are not. Then the next thing we will hear is that your family will be joining you wherever you will be, but for that to happen you will have married a gay man."

"What is 'gay'?" I had asked. Not because I did not know, but because I did not understand. I had been reminded that I rarely used Facebook because I was always busy searching Google for scholarships—scholarships in the United States of America, in Sweden and Japan, and in Canada and Australia. But I had never asked Google who exactly provides those scholarships and what their main intentions are. I had never asked Google what brain drain is, and whether it is real or a social construct, the new nightmare that I was beginning to understand. I had never asked Google what would happen to me if I got a scholarship, whether it would be just to go and study, or to go and study and work, or to go and study and work and marry a gay man. Thinking about this scared me! Deep inside I felt empty and helpless, but I whispered to myself that I was also trying to understand that it's all about time. Just time. And that became my highlight of volunteering at the biogas project.

When I heard of this new construction to be done, reflex brought me back to that conversation. Talking about this motivated Alberto, Sugabo, and I to join *Babe* Dlamini. He had another Swazi apprentice with whom we had to work closely. The rest of the youth had refused, denying being exploited as usual. But the three of us knew well that above money, there is also joy in making small contributions to building the community, and we took on the challenge.

It wasn't long before we set to work. Our first task was to use buckets to remove all the rainwater that had accumulated in the large rectangular pits after a recent storm. Emptying more than a hundred and fifty cubic meters of water using a small bucket was quite the task. We then started mixing cement and sand, fetched bricks that were to make the internal walls and the base, and we built everything from scratch. The contract was to work for eight hours per day for each of the work days, and we would be paid 1000 rands all together regardless of how long the work took. Our families were probably more enthusiastic about the money than we were, because it meant they would be able to afford soap and salt as well as our school supplies for the next academic year.

Most of what I remember of the experience are beautiful conversations with Alberto and Sugabo, New Year's resolutions to look forward to, and, to a lesser extent, skills.

We deconstructed our sorrow and glued the pieces of our hearts together with realistic hopes. One conversation sticks out in particular: we realized that we all wanted to go to Waterford Kamhlaba, the United World College of Southern Africa. We promised each other that we would do all it took to go there, realizing that it was the only way to get a scholarship, and probably the only way to escape the refugee life, the life that had wearied us to the best of its ability. For one, that dream would come true. For another, it would be modified, because fate would resettle him in Denmark. For yet other, it would remain just a dream, kept at arm's length by an unforgiving reality. Little did we know what lay ahead of us, but *hope* had always been a spark to ignite some light, and dreams had become the manufacturer of *hope.*

After we started the third term of school, everyone became busy—or at least we all tried to be. Even those who had neglected school in the beginning seemed to sink into the books. I thought it would be hard to pass the exams that tested the two-year-long curricula in just one month. I always observed and smiled, because I knew I was on top of the game. In my efforts to help, I started spending more and more time at school. Combined with my duties as the Head Boy of the school and the chairperson of the Youth Club, this became the busiest time of my academic year.

School usually let out ten minutes before 4 p.m., but I usually stayed until 6 p.m. trying to help those I could. We worked on physics, chemistry, biology, geography, and mathematics, mostly because those subjects were where most of the students were struggling. Zazi, the class monitor, Zenani, the deputy Head Girl, and myself were on the forefront. Soon enough we had formed study groups. Those of us who were living within a walkable radius from the school commuted there at night as well, and I used my badge to secure a classroom for the Form 5 students

I would wake up at 4:55 a.m. and do a short prayer. By 5:15 a.m. I was ready for school, and I worked until *pakela,* or 6:50 a.m. when I headed to school. Often, I left for school on an empty stomach because *pakela* was sometimes delayed. The day was transient, and my routine sent me to bed around midnight. I had a timetable and all that I did was perfectly planned, except when the classmates at school expressed a wish to change our schedule.

Mark and Katherine were a couple volunteering with the Peace Corps who had come to Mpaka a year before. Their main goal was to fight the spread of HIV/AIDS, mainly targeting young people in schools including Mpaka High School, Malindza Primary School, and Mpaka Railway Primary school.

However, during this critical time of the academic year, Mark and Katherine were helping students in any way they could. They had devised a daily "word of the day" program that they delivered on the morning assemblies, which meant that they were at school as early as the assembly time. They gave workshops about HIV and AIDS, demonstrated how to properly use a condom, and assisted in English lessons for any teachers who were interested. I remember a day when Mark was invited into my literature class to help us discuss Shakespeare's Sonnet 116, "Let me not to the true marriage of minds," and his first remark was that literature was not something that he ever studied in depth, although he had read many books. But he did all he could to help us understand the Elizabethan English and advised us on different aspects of interpreting poetry. "Focus on the image the poet is trying to paint," he had said, "that will help you to discern the central message." They were always ready to help academically and socially; they had grown fond of young people from the refugee camp. We had invited them to participate in our Youth Club activities on a number of occasions, and through their work both at Mpaka High School and at Malindza Primary school they sympathized with the struggles of young refugees. They were particularly touched by our inability to attain our fullest academic potential due to the language barrier.

The couple and I became closer and closer through our interactions at school: in class, whenever they needed my assistance as the Head Boy, on different sports and competition trips, and in the camp when they would come to visit the Youth Club or the primary school children whom they cherished so much. Little did I know that every time we interacted, they listened to my sighs and, reserved though I was, they tried to understand my heart's desires. They had invited me to have lunch with them at their place, which was not very far away from the school; to talk to their children back in Washington DC, to greet their friends who came to visit them. Could it be that they had a greater vision for me?

They were always near me. During the times when we were preparing for exams, I started asking them questions about education in the United States, specifically about the possibility of getting a scholarship. Their answer was always the same: "From a rural school like this, and the Swazi education level, it is very hard, even impossible, to get a place in any American institution." But I kept pressing, and they kept researching without my knowledge. We talked about high schools in the United States, bridging programs, and so on. One day they told me about a school in South Africa that would greatly enhance my passion for Africa: the African Leadership Academy (ALA). They had heard it from a friend who heard from a friend who was a friend of a friend working there. When they explained this to me, with their strong United States accent that they always tried to simplify by slowing down in their speech, I smiled and told them that there were many "friend" levels involved. I was very happy that they were passing this information to a friend who might find it very useful.

The minute we parted, I went straight to the computer lab. We rarely had access to it, but as the Head Boy of the school, I had greater access to facilities than most. I typed "African Leadership Academy" into Google and read all that I could find for the entire afternoon. It was amazing! Within the next few days and weeks, I had printed three copies of the application form and was working with Mark and Katherine to fill it out.

Mabha, one of my classmates, lived at Mpaka Railway Station. His father worked for the company, and they had a large apartment. He approached me sometimes around break time and asked me to join him and live with him there, but I laughed, thinking that he was making fun of me—he liked to do that. But in this case, he wasn't. He needed somebody to motivate him to study and to help him in academics, and I was that someone. Besides, I needed a place to stay too—where I could be alone, free from the noise of the camp and with good lights—so that I could fully concentrate on studying. I would not need to worry about food, because it would be provided for both of us. This sounded indeed like a wonderful offer, but I wasn't the only one in class who could be his study partner. After all, there were other classmates like Ziyanda, the Head Girl, and Zazi, the class monitor. Why of all people would he think of me? Besides, I had my family to think about—my father and I being the only men of the house. I had to fetch water and be there for my nieces. Maybe the Youth Club would not be a problem because I could always go back to the camp on Friday evenings for the meetings, and on Saturdays for the cleaning activities. But what about the evening study sessions that I had initiated and had to oversee, to ensure that the hall cautiously provided by the camp administration was being used appropriately, and that the kids were indeed studying? I thanked him for the offer and told him that I would think about it. He said he would be willing to come down to the camp and talk to my father if he had to, and I found that courageous—he had never been in the camp before.

He did not really need to talk to anyone, because if I decided that I wanted to join him, my family would not stop me. I was privileged to have the liberty to make my own decisions—something for which I will forever thank my parents. But I was willing to test how far he would go with his request, and I asked him to visit.

I decided I would live with him, and this was the first time I would live outside Mpaka Refugee Camp. It felt good! The beautiful gardens and tranquility of Mpaka Railway Village were exactly what I needed. There were many different avenues that in the following weeks proved to be wonderful for the combination of my new hobby of jogging, and there was a clear, soothing breeze. As soon as I relocated there, taking with me only my guitar, my books, and a handful of clothes, I was received not only by Mabha but by other classmates who lived in the village, as well as Form 5 students from other schools. That's when

I understood that it was a set up! They possibly wanted me to lead a study group, and Mabha and his friends secured a classroom for every evening at Mpaka Railway Primary School. Night walks to Mpaka High School were greatly reduced to almost no walk, and we asked other classmates who wanted to join us to also come to Mpaka Railway. Then the party started: gearing up for the final exams. But there was one tiny problem on my part.

Ever since I declined to learn and write siSwati for my SGCSE, I had chosen to learn French, which was based on the International General Certificate for Secondary Education curriculum. The Ministry of Education required us to learn two languages. French was not taught at school, so I had to make that arrangement myself. The only thing the school would help me was to organize my trip to Siteki Nazarene, a high school in Siteki, where I could do the French oral examinations because they taught the language and had a teacher who qualified for testing. I had only one resource: my father.

Since the start of the third term we had started French lessons that he drafted himself, having no knowledge of what the syllabus required. But together, we decided that he would prepare me and I would pass French with flying colors. Later, I researched online and found the syllabus, and through connections of the students at Siteki Nazarene I borrowed the prescribed book for the syllabus, and then we were properly on board.

Living away from home meant that my father and I had to plan well the place and time for the lessons. After some thinking, we agreed to meet halfway: I would remain at school after classes and he would come to tutor me there.

I secured a classroom, and we would have lessons and leave the school together. Parting with him outside the school premises always haunted my mind.

He was nearing the verge of fragility. I saw him carry a small bag that he pretended had books in it. I imagined the silent sorrow that he bore with patience and perseverance—life. I always looked at him as we parted, and wondered how I would ever repay his love, his care, his incomparable motivation. He would turn away and head back to the camp while I pretended to head to toward the shopping complex on my way to Swaziland Railway. But I would stand, as if paralyzed, watching him as he faded farther and farther from view. He was doing his best he could to help me to be a person—the most valuable gift a son can inherit from a father.

One day, while looking at him, motionless, I started imagining other situations of young people in the camp: those who were their own parents and had no one to motivate them to have dreams, let alone to pursue them like me. Those whose role models were drunkards who found themselves in trouble all the time. Those who took after the men whose only ways to get a drink (not even a meal for the family) were to steal other people's property, commit fraud, and so on. There were many who had lost opportunities due to the mobile lives we led, and their parents did not seem to care. My father, unlike the others, always regretted the opportunities I had missed due to being on the run.

I slowly sauntered toward Mpaka Railway. I could not help but think about that scene. The more I thought about it, the more I wanted to think of it. My hero, my dad. I made a promise to myself that I told him later, and he challenged me to keep it.

When I arrived at the house I checked for the secret place where Mabha and I had agreed to keep the key, and I entered. I looked at my guitar patiently waiting for me in the corner and I started to pluck the strings. They were as melancholic as I was, and our interaction resulted in a beautiful melody that later became a song. I entitled it "The Light."

October came swiftly. The drought was severe—thank God my parents had given up any attempts to farm after the experience from the previous year. My father tended only a small garden where he grew eggplants for sale. In return, this complemented my sister's hassle. Every Wednesday and Thursday she went to Manzini to sell secondhand clothes that were imported from Maputo. Her work supported our family. We lived on.

"Ola ese," Zazi hollered to me. We had just met up on the morning of Thursday, the sixth of November. We were starting our walk to Mpaka High to write our second geography paper.

"Hey man. What's up?"

"Nothing much Mr. Jones." He liked to call me Mr. Jones, after the character in George Orwell's *Animal Farm*. I never really understood why that particular name appealed to him, but I enjoyed it. "I finish the exams today!" He asserted.

"Matoootaaa!" Mabha interjected in a very high-pitched tone, a form of surprise. I looked at them both. I still had

French six days later. I was the only French student, and the school had arranged to find a room for me—the only refugee who survived to reach Form 5, to successfully graduate in Mpaka High School's class of 2014. The rest had either dropped out or failed and had to repeat Form 4. Two of the dropouts had gotten pregnant and had left the refugee camp in absolute secrecy. In a split second, as Zazi and Mabha exclaimed their excitement at finishing their exams, I had thought about all this and the realization that I was the only remaining student from the camp caught me off guard. My first reaction was to walk across the street to the other side of the walkway. Both Mabha and Zazi stared at me but continued their exhilarated chit-chat. I stared down at the ground for the next approximately two hundred meters without saying a word to anyone on the other side of the road. I had so much going on inside my brain!

"Mr. Jones?" Zazi called me loudly, as they all burst into laughter, startling me. I looked straight at him as if I had just woken up from a dream.

"What, what???"

"We were just talking here: What is your favorite memory that you'll take from our class—Mpaka High School Class of 2014?"

"I don't know," I said after a long pause. Slowly and softly, I forced my voice out. Again, my brain went completely blank for a moment, and all I could see ahead of me was a greyish-white haze that seemed to accumulate more and more at every passing millisecond. "*Ma-ani*, wait a second: Do, you remember the trip we had to South Africa? Crossing the border legally for the first time will always be memorable to me."

I don't know why I singled out this exact moment out of all my two years at Mpaka. It wasn't fun at all. Just like my friends, it also took me a long time to understand what I had just said. This was a trip to Mpumalanga Province that the school had organized. We had visited Kruger National Park to learn about ecological sustainability and continued to the Sudwala caves—caves set in Precambrian dolomite rock that conceal a fascinating history that goes back to thousands of millions of years ago. We had spent the night at the banks of Sabie River and the following morning had explored other famous tourist spots like the Three Rondavels—three mountains shaped like historical African style huts—God's Window, the Lone Creek Falls, and the city of Nelspruit. I had enjoyed this trip more than anything, but whatever joy I had across the Matsamo border post seemed meaningless in relation to the unexplainable feeling of having legally crossed the border for the first time in my life.

All the way from the DRC, through Rwanda to Tanzania, through Tanzania to Malawi, from Malawi through Mozambique to Swaziland—we did not have proper documentation papers—thanks to Smuggler the Almighty we managed, but often we had to use more informal ways. We had to brave snakes and other wild animals. We had to mount the cliffs, cross valleys and outwit the raging waters of rivers or lakes. The worst had been braving armed soldiers or rebels ...

... When I crossed Matsamo using a refugee travel document that Home Affairs had grudgingly provided me, I had a flashback of all that I had to go through with my family, and my mind became more overshadowed by the cruelty that ignited all the troubles we live. I wished I could find a place to cry, but there was none. And I couldn't get myself to cry. I pretended to feel like one of the class, but at that very same moment the façade vanished, leaving me feeling naked and lonely.

I attempted to explain all this to my friends, and all they could do was to give back exaggerated nods, pretending to understand me. I smiled ironically, and we trod on. We went to Mpaka to write their very last exam; the second-to-last exam for me.

The examinations were done before I knew it, and a few weeks after that Mabha left Mpaka Railway for a long visit to his relatives in a different town. I went back to the refugee camp—where I belonged. In the camp, things were falling apart.

CHAPTER 5:

FALSE AWAKENING

I finished high school. Thanks to Mark and Katherine, I had submitted my application form for the A-levels at St. Marks High School and sat for the entrance exams two weeks after writing the national exams. I waited with absolute certainty that I would get a place there. Mark and Katherine had paid for all the costs, involved, including exam fees and transport, and assured me that they would take care of the tuition and hostel fees if I got in. They just didn't want to see my brain degenerating in the camp after completing Form 5 like those of many other young people. I always feel blessed to have met them.

Meanwhile, I was working tirelessly on the application form to the African Leadership Academy, a Pan-African school situated in the outskirts of Johannesburg, South

Africa that aims to transform the African continent through educating and developing future leaders. The ALA application spoke directly to my desire to see change in Africa. But no matter how much I tried to focus on the future—my future—more awaited me in the camp: horror, and experiences that forced me to be the adult of the family.

Before I left the camp to live with Mabha in September, there had been some significant changes. The Ministry of Home Affairs had managed to convince the refugees of the need to renovate Titanic, and that it wouldn't take long—whatever that might mean. They had set up UNHCR tents in some of the farms in the side of the camp as temporary residences for all those who were living in Titanic. It never gets better!

When I returned to the camp people had adapted. Young children were running all around in their nakedness and innocence. Teens were dressing up neatly, trying hard to look polished for their peers despite not noticing the discrepancy between their looks and their residences. Mothers cooked evening meals in friends' houses (because you couldn't really cook in a tent, and using the open area outside was not an option—lest a neighbor's kid ran into your pot and overturned it or an enemy dropped some undesirable chemicals in your soup when you looked away!), and they still assaulted their misbehaving or annoying young ones with so much love and care, avoiding doing so during the clear daylight or late in the night for obvious reasons. Men roamed around joylessly or tried to occupy their minds with senseless conversations. Life had gained some sense of normalcy.

Two weeks later, everything changed. In the early morning of Saturday, the twenty-second of November, someone saw the need to disrupt the peace that was prevailing in the impoverished minds. One of the tents was set ablaze.

The dim light from zealous flames struggled to overcome the intense darkness. The popping sounds of burning plastic and other materials trapped inside the tents succeeded in overcoming the loud silence that had fallen in the previous few hours of the night. This, soon enough, merged with horrid cries here and there as everyone in the camp (including the camp officials) woke up to witness the traumatic sight. The smoke filled the atmosphere while horror suffocated each one of us, but we all had two concerns: Was the family all right? Who did this? The confusion that befell our small lower world was certainly confusing; the malice had done what it intended.

The tent that was set ablaze had hosted a Rwandan mother and her six children. Only after much water was wasted in the failed attempt to put out the fire did everyone notice that outside stood a horrified mother and five of her children. The sixth child, a five-year-old boy, lay in the remaining ashes, the black skin turned blacker as a result of the combustion, but with some slimy segments of flesh scattered all over the body. He was barely breathing his last molecules of air, and his heartbeat was fading fast as if bidding farewell to this cruel world. This sparked another round of horrid cries later in the morning as the innocent child was confirmed dead by the Good Shepherd Hospital in Siteki. The camp entered a period of mourning.

One week later the child was buried amid all the confusion the world could offer. Everyone, including my own family members, was traumatized. Those who had history with fires, like my own family, were so restless that the nights turned into nightmares, and sleeplessness became the new fashion.

Three weeks after the incident, when everyone thought life was beginning to return to normal, another tent was set on fire. The same atmosphere, the same horrid cries, but luckily there was no one in the tent. It belonged to a single Burundian man, thirty years old, and although booze is highly criticized, it saved his life. He had fallen asleep elsewhere due to his inability to stagger his way home (at least that's the official story) and around 3 a.m. he was among the spectators of his tent's animated flames. He couldn't recover even his underpants or his favorite picture that sparked the memories of his roots. This occurred the night of Tuesday, December 10.

The next night was even more horrifying than its two predecessors. Yet another tent was set ablaze, this time hosting the whole family—a Congolese family. They were caught unexpectedly, probably well aware of this recurring catastrophe since it was now general knowledge that the camp was not safe anymore, but unable to help it. A husband, his wife and their five children were clustered in two small tents merged into one. Their twelve-year-old daughter died right away, as she was trapped in some sort of garments inside and could not be saved, and her elder sister still bears the marks of second-degree burns all over her body.

Each of the two little lost lives left emotional lacerations, as did surviving girl who became a perpetual reminder of the horrific acts. We wondered when the instigator would be found, as was publicly promised by the police force, and even now we are still wondering.

The Swazi Royal Police posted some officers to patrol the camp day and night after the third incident. We also wondered where they had been all along, but in answer to this question, we realized that we were refugees. An 8 p.m. curfew was instituted for all the refugees. All those who had relocated to the tents were given the main hall to sleep in.

They lived in the tents during the day and slept in the hall during the night. This was the same hall that had been built for important official meetings, and that we had secured for studying and for Youth Club activities, but it instantly became a sleeping place.

There were husbands and their snoring sons, mothers and their crying babies. The stench was impressive—from the abundance of flatus expelled in sleep, from the children releasing themselves in sleep, from the odor of those who had not bathed in ages (mainly to save water), from the smoke trapped in clothes during the day's cooking, and so on. There was the insecurity of sleeping next to someone you had insulted few weeks before, or even a member of a different nationality. There were many things to haunt the traumatized! Many did not sleep, but rather *meditated* every long night until dawn. Then at dawn they gathered their tattered belongings and headed back to the tents where they would lay their heads.

The police could protect the refugees from the malice in the outer world, but the malice in the inner minds and hearts recurred now more than ever, and once more, depression reigned. Fewer interactions; more sobs, anger, and hostility. People did not see eye to eye. Anyone you accidentally looked in the eyes clenched their teeth. Now that I think about it, this place had all characteristics of Hell.

Fear spread in the entire camp like a wildfire, or as cholera would in impoverished communities. It assimilated into everyone's thoughts and memory. It probed the long unforgotten memories, stimulated yet another round of hopelessness. Who was burning the tents? Were the people chased from Titanic and cast into the tents to be burned? We never stopped wondering.

Theories had started to arise: maybe the Rwandan diaspora was working after all. The Rwandan government was known to send spies who would severely punish specific Hutu refugee families, and for these acts to be concealed, some lives from other nationalities had to be sacrificed. Perhaps some refugees wanted the United Nations to come back and rescue us from the incapable Swazi government, and there must always be a sacrifice for a good cause. People's abhorrence for each other had grown so much that some people were clearly expressing to others what they were capable of. Nobody knew what was what, but clearly the camp became even more divided. Congolese men clustered together far apart from everyone else. Burundians visited only Burundians. The Rwandans tried to be neutral by minding their own business, while Somalians continued to worship Allah as Somalians and remained in their circle.

Likewise, young people had to follow instructions from their elders.

Whether in the hall or in the houses, sleeplessness was everywhere. I realized that perhaps it was time to return the favor to my horrified, sleep deprived family. I decided to spend the nights awake and sleep in the morning. That would least arouse some hope and trick my family into feeling that they were protected. My father objected at first, but I was stubborn enough that he eventually gave in. After all, was I not the one who, back in the nights when I was young, stood outside our humble building and watched the stars hanging freely up there, while at the same time I keenly observed the bats coming from the attic? Did I not chase the shiny ladybugs before my mum sent around workers to come and force me to sleep? This time I wanted to be like those lovely nocturnal beings. I had never wanted it before, but life forced me to desire it, crave it like I craved for life itself. At least the bats and the beetles were free for the night. They flew from house to house, tree to tree, bush to bush with much easy and pleasure. No pressure. I was forced to be a non-hooting night owl, hunting for the peace of mind that had deserted all. The night shrieks of those who had lost beloved ones had painted a large, dark emptiness at the core of my heart like never before. They had resuscitated the dark memories of my childhood, those which I had never understood until life hit me. They had walked right into me, and freely asked me if I was up to growth, up to manliness.

Living in hell, I had to sustain the fire. I had to quench the ever-growing fear, and I bet many young people did, if not for their fathers, mothers or siblings, for themselves. We had no other option.

Every time I looked into the eyes of my nieces who still fell asleep at normal times, I imagined what it was like to be so innocent and so carefree. And the idea itself was scared away by the specter of what it would be to lose either or both of them. It was time to man up.

I first had to assure my frail mother that it would be all right, that should there be a need to wake up everyone I would do it in a split second. If the house were to be set ablaze, I would quickly scream to the top of my voice, seize my two nieces, and run outside. My father understood all that I wanted, which was for everyone who slept under that roof to feel at ease, at peace, and cared for. I had no idea whether I was prepared enough to convince my body to let me do this though, for circadian rhythms can be harsh sometimes. But I knew it is always possible, for I had heard of the people who fly across many times zones and can still adjust and function properly. I knew some people who were doctors and nurses before life hit them hard, that sometimes they had night shifts. This was my time to have night shifts.

I began my night watch the night of the fifteenth of December. Other than staying awake, I had not planned anything tangible to do during this night, so I just did what came to my mind. At first, I communed quietly with my guitar, who sustained my improvisation. Then everyone slept and I stopped playing music. Around midnight I started arranging the messy things in my room: books, clothes, and broken phone chargers—all that I owned. Later on, I opened my laptop and started playing games from *Microsoft Student with Encarta Premium* like

Geography Quiz, as well as computer games like Chess Titans. I switched through programs like Adobe Photoshop and Adobe Soundbooth, all of which appeared in the three-quarter-intact portion of the laptop screen. Thank God I had this old, rugged, dilapidated laptop! It was so old and broken that it made a peculiar buzzing sounds because of vibrations of broken parts caused by its rotating cooling fun, and my close friends baptized it Mosquito. It kept me company, helped me throughout my studying in Forms 4 and 5. I had inherited it from my father, who had received it from a friend who had no use for it when we were still in Malawi. The laptop had turned out to be a great friend, and now I needed it more than ever. I spent the night juggling different activities, all of which I thought were beneficial to me. I slept at 4 a.m., just when the darkness was slowly giving way to light.

I had to wake up at 7 a.m., however, being the leader of the Youth Club, because there was a Christmas campaign organized by the Taiwan Fund for Children and Families and the Youth Club had an integral role to play. I woke up, I staggered, feeling like a drunkard—I was incredibly tired, with a headache as if I had a serious hangover. This triggered my meditation. *What is life really?* But it reminded me that I had to be strong if I ever wanted to find answers.

In the morning, the sun shone as usual, but I slept again shortly after meeting the youth and delegating a few activities—who was to receive the visitors, to arrange the tables and benches in the hall, to monitor the kids, to carry stuff that will need to be carried, and so on. The campaign itself turned out to be amazing, with many infants (whose parents were bold enough to let them attend) seeming very happy to be there. I returned to bed, and I did not get to see the sun shining until past midday when it was as scorching as the horrific fires that had forced me into staying the nights awake. It shined over the leftover ashes from the fires that had consumed the tents in the preceding days, shined so ominously that I wondered whether the world itself were not going to be set ablaze. This thought clouded my mind; I hated humanity and I wished to see the day when we would all burn instead of some suffering and others not caring.

The next night I kept watch like the previous one, but this night was different. Nature communicated with me.

Now that I knew how it felt to stay up the entire night, I had planned to do many things during my sleepless nights. I did not want to just spend the nights watching, waiting for no one and doing nothing at all. When fate hits you, you often have to respond with courage and the strong motivation to transform it into opportunity. That is what I did. Having Mosquito, I knew I could watch movies that would keep me engaged and learning. I had numerous novels to read, even besides *The Complete Works of William Shakespeare* that I had borrowed from my former literature teacher. I had been given a book to summarize, *Our Journey Together,* by a priest who occasionally came to the camp to celebrate mass with the few of us who still had faith in the Catholic Church. I had my music skills to improve, although ideally I was not supposed to make noise during the night. I had an endless desire to do whatever it took to make myself a better person, and I would not have wanted to waste these precious hours of the night doing just nothing. Even if I was afraid, petrified, and anxious about whether my family and I will see the next rays or not, the tranquility of the night embedded in the loneliness and the fear that besieged me was not to go unaddressed.

I also promised myself to dedicate 3 a.m. to the Lord Almighty, my hope and my motivation. My source of strength in the journey of life. I would do everything else, stop at 3 a.m. to recite the Holy Rosary and other prayers, which would take me toward 4 a.m., then spend a few more minutes detecting whether there was any movement in the camp; and if there were, I would take notice of it and decide whether to wait for few more minutes until daybreak or whether I could sleep.

These two first nights, whenever I heard a slightly unusual noise, I rushed to the so-called living room, peeped through the window, looked around, and then headed back to my tiny room. And by unusual noise, it could be anything! I was as alert as a cat hunting for mice in the house, and this led me to an exciting episode.

I have grown to believe in miracles and not magic nor superstition. On the second night, I was visited, and I confirmed right away that it was a message from above. As I was still struggling to find the right combinations of activities to do during these dark days and darker nights, on the second night I continued watching the second season of *The Good Wife,* a legal series from the United States I had begun watching on Mosquito. When the time neared 3 a.m., I did not feel like praying, and I decided just to continue watching Alicia Florrick do her things. However, it happened that at 3 a.m. sharp I unconsciously looked at the time and instantaneously at my rosary, promptly grabbed it, paused my VLC media player and went on with the prayer. I felt extremely peaceful. It was like tranquility had seized the throne at that very instant.

As I was in prayer, several events took place. My niece coughed, and my mother (probably in her sleep or even awake) told me to go and check if she was covered in the blankets. I went to check and kind of startled my sister, who rose in her sleep, her heart thumping in the most unusual manner I have ever felt, and asked breathlessly, "What happened?" only to hear a very soft, calming voice from me saying, "It's all good, I just came to see if the child is covered." I covered her properly and went back to my den.

A few minutes later, I heard a strange noise. It was some kind of dull sound from friction, just a thud, yet I pictured flames and the combustive noise they produce. I hurried to the sitting room, scanned the kitchen, peeped through the window panes; there was nothing unusual. I later figured out it was just a person or two from the family we shared the house with who was turning restlessly in bed. I decided to sit in the living room as I proceeded to my prayer. I was trying to focus, asking God relentlessly that those malevolent people who robbed our peace and brought the past even closer to us would be captured by the police, at least for restoration of calmness and hope in refugees' souls.

As I sat with my rosary in my hands and my focus on Jesus and the Blessed Virgin Mary, I looked in front of me and my gaze met that of a large frog that appeared very dark. I immediately paused the prayer, trying to figure out what to do. I am naturally fond of animals, so I wasn't afraid or scared, but how was I to deal with this uninvited guest? How did it enter the house in the first place?

My greatest fear in trying to get rid of this frog, amid the utter silence—the dead of the night—was to unintentionally arouse the sleepers as if there were some form of danger. My small brain worked its magic, and soon I devised a plan which worked quite well.

I took a *kitenge*, a rectangular piece of fabric that women wear, holding it in my left hand since in the right hand I was still holding my rosary. I think it sensed my intention, because it tried to run away and find refuge under the table. I spread the *kitenge* over the frog and slowly lowered it; I managed to grab it with ease when it hopped away, wrapping it in the garment and holding it in my palm.

I wanted to throw it outside but I did not. Opening the door could evoke suspicion that I was somehow associated with the evildoers. The police were presumably patrolling the camp, and I wouldn't risk them seeing me. I then decided to take it to my room and keep it until the morning. I reached my room, sat down, finished the glorious mysteries of the rosary and then turned my attention back to the visitor, who now became my hostage.

I feared the frog might suffocate with how I was clutching it, so I tried to increase its free space within the *kitenge*. After doing this I tied the cloth with my phone charger's long wire, put it on my study table, and put two books on top of the cloth so that the frog would be trapped but not uncomfortable. But soon I noticed that it was trying to free itself! Besides, it would move slowly with the cloth, and if I did not keep motionless it would make noise, which I clearly did not want.

I resumed watching The Good Wife, pretending not to pay any attention to it. But a few minutes later, I lost concentration and started thinking about the frog again. I paused the video and stared at it, wrapped inside that piece of cloth.

It had been caught in the night, in the dark. It was trying hard but had been unable to free itself. Its freedom would come in the morning, with the first light, because I, the mighty controller, had decided so. Could there be a parallel between this sacred frog and myself?

Politics, wars, discrimination, racism, refugee life, xenophobia, and many more—my night. I had been trying to free myself through education and hard work, my struggles for survival, but there seemed to be no way out. Was it all part of a deific masterpiece? Thinking about this made me momentarily oblivious about the second part of my epiphany, and my heart beat so much faster and harder that I could almost feel my ribs falling off my chest.

A few minutes past 4 a.m. I released the frog and watched it leap and hop to freedom, taking its time, jumping a step at a time. It seemed to be an auspicious omen: I was to see the light some day!

All the traumatic incidents in November and early December had left my family shaken, and we unanimously decided that it was best to get out of the refugee camp. My sister promised my parents that she would do whatever it took to raise money to get us out of the camp, but this was easier said than done. My two elder brothers and elder sister had left already. They had all dropped out of school almost a year before to look for work to support the family. I was the only one in school, and this had come with a significant responsibility: to do the best I could, to be the best I could be. And here I was, the only person who could possibly move out of the camp and interact with the locals in my poor and broken siSwati. Especially because I had had many trips—for sports, debates, science and math competitions—I had a deeper understanding of the country than my father or any other family member did. My sister and I agreed with my father that I would start my quest to find cheap accommodation outside of the refugee camp, and that my sister would do her best to increase her sales in the second-hand-clothes business.

I did not know where to start. And it was even harder because we had to do the search in complete secrecy. Transportation was expensive, so I had to walk whenever I could. Leaving as early as 7 a.m., I targeted the major shopping centers and squatter settlements. There you could always interact with different people and get an overview of where there might be houses to rent. My father had told me to consider three main factors in my hunting. First, the house should cost little yet be big enough to accommodate the whole family. Second, it would preferably be in an agricultural area where we could have a small farm. Third, it would ideally be as far away and secluded from the camp as possible. The third factor made it difficult because the farther away the house was, the greater the distance needed for transportation and the harder it would be to move the few possessions that we had. But I was determined to do this service for my family, and I embarked on endless journeys in search of a new home.

Often my father would come with me, and whenever we got a lead, I would do all the directing and talking while he did all the observing. I enjoyed spending more time alone with him and having father–son talks. Places like Moneni and Fairview in Manzini, as well as Kwaluseni in Matsapa, had affordable houses, but these were either located in the most informal settlements, where sanitation and social amenities were unheard of, or they were too small. After a few visits to such places another fourth factor was added: I had to look for a place that was situated within a walkable distance to a kindergarten and a primary school. In my parents' minds, I wasn't a problem anymore: I was seventeen and had finished high school. But there were my two nieces to think of, for whom getting out of the camp meant moving away from school. I respected that, but it complicated the search even more.

From Mpaka, in the eastern part of the country, we had to look past Mbabane, looking as far as Piggs Peak in the far northwest. Every day it became more and more complicated. My sister was working hard to cover the transport costs, but our resources were becoming exhausted. I was not sleeping anymore, because I was always thinking of the other possible places that I could look. We had been directed to some mud-and-grass houses, often with just two rooms, no kitchen, and no bathroom in the clusters of squatter settlements, and often we had been tempted to rent them, but my father always thought of my nieces' upbringing and my mother's frailty. We had almost given up hope when I received a phone call from a place we had visited a few weeks before.

In one of my visits to Malkerns, we had found a house which met all the criteria but did not have an owner. The previous owners had divorced, and the neighbors did not know whether the house belonged to the wife or to the husband. I left our phone number just in case the wife or husband showed up. Neither did, but a short distance away there was a closed compound and the tenants in one of the houses had moved away a month before. The landlord had heard of the hopeless characters who had been running up and down Malkerns and had called us.

We soon found a perfect match for our needs, and I then had to worry about organizing a truck for transportation. We indicated to the camp officials that we were to relocate from the camp soon—an idea that was happily received but at the same time poignant because the camp officials had grown fond of my family.

"Hey there," I greeted.

"Hey," she answered, with a disguised smile. It was as if she were always preserving her smile for something, or rather someone special. I loved that about her. As usual, it had been days since we last had water in the camp, and the management had been compelled to provide tanked water. We were the only two people remaining at the water tanks, between the kitchen where they cooked *pakela* and the clinic. It was raining lightly.

"So, it seems like it's me and you. The two of us alone. Together."

"Thanks to the rain, I guess."

"Not really though." I liked to challenge Keza with arguments every time we were together. For some reasons unknown to me, I thought it was a great way of getting her to talk. She wasn't as shy as other girls, and we interacted more often than perhaps our parents would have wanted, but I loved arguing with her.

"What do you mean not really? Ah! This boy!"

"Well, you do realize that a lot of people had finished fetching water before the first raindrops made their way down, right?"

"Hmmm, sure. But haven't you fetched as well? Why are you here?"

"Hey ho, hold on! No attitude," I teased, looking at her keenly. "I'm here for you. [Pause] No, just kidding! You know water always appears and disappears from time to time, so now that we got a chance of getting the tank opened, I might as well store as much water as I can. Especially now that Kikongo is afraid of the rain, and I have all the freedom in the world."

"You are here for me, eh?" She was looking down, shaking her head softly and periodically when she said this. I was astonished that my words had stuck.

"Yeah. That as well!" By now she had filled her four containers. I walked closer and lifted one of the containers to put in my wheelbarrow. My family was one of the few to have bought a wheelbarrow because we always had to travel out of the camp to fetch water, and in the initial days when my brother and I had to carry containers with our hands it was entirely too hectic. Many families relied on the men of the house, which was the case for me until very recently.

"Wha-aat are you doing?" She asked, looking at me sternly this time. I did not answer, but instead I approached the tap and took the second container. As I was about to lift it and place it properly in the wheelbarrow, she grabbed my hand. Her touch sent a strange wave of liveliness in my body. I looked at her and smiled.

"Let me …" was all I said. I pushed the wheelbarrow and dropped the two containers at her house, came back and made a second round to fetch her remaining containers.

All this was done in utter silence and with the exchange of smiles. What a young lady she was! Her good-natured heart stood out in how she was always there for her friends, dispersing joy through her singing and dancing talents and all our sweet interactions. She was beautiful. I was taken in by her elegance when she walked or posed while sitting down, her half-smiles that barely registered on her adorable lips, her poise, her impeccable natural dark complexion, her soft-spoken nature. She was one of a kind, and my heart filled with sadness when it crossed my mind that I would leave her!

When I returned after dropping off all her containers, half my containers were already filled with water, staring at me from two meters away from the tap. She asked me to finish the rest, as she walked up to her house without saying more. Within five minutes she was back, carrying a plastic basin that had clothing in it. I had just finished when she sat down and positioned herself to get some water she would use to wash the clothes. I sat on one of my containers, and we continued talking.

After about half an hour or so, as the rain raged more and more, my father appeared from a distance. The moment he noticed the two of us he slowed down but walked on toward us. I thought he might have been a bit worried, wondering where I disappeared to in the rain. He asked how we were doing, to which I told him I would be home soon, and he turned around without saying much. Meanwhile Keza had condensed herself, trying to shrink into an ant or just be swallowed by the ground altogether. I laughed, and she slapped me softly on the cheek. I felt her gentle palm, further smoothened by the washing soap she used. But the conversation that followed changed the tender atmosphere.

"Keza, there is something I have to tell you."

"Alright, what is it?"

"I'm leaving. I'm leaving the camp."

"So what?" She might have thought I was joking at first. But my lack of direct response compelled her to narrow down the possibilities.

"You look serious. Are you?" Her tone was somehow inflected by disbelief. In our conversation we had talked about love extensively. She had been explaining to me how weird we, the guys, were and had convinced me how we knew nothing about how to treat a lady. Obviously, I had to be the man and stand up for my gender. The passionate manner in which we argued concealed some inner desires, and we both knew it, but neither of us wanted to break the ice. Perhaps it wasn't the right time. Thinking about this also added more weight to my words, and I felt a rush of emotions that I struggled to control.

"There is also something else I have to tell you."

"Wait, I don't understand."

"There is only one thing you need to understand."

"And that would be …?"

"I want you to know that I love you. And that I will always love you!"

"…"

"I have arranged a truck that will move the whole family on the twenty-eighth of December. Please don't tell anyone. I will come back on the 31st to celebrate the New Year with you and the Youth Club."

"What do you mean you are leaving?"

"Please don't tell anyone. Okay? I love you."

Sibonginkhosi Dlamini, Sifiso Mbokhazi, and I learned that we had been selected as the three finalists to go to the African Leadership Academy campus in early January, and we had to start preparing for the trip right away. I had less than three weeks to apply for the South African visa. The other two didn't have to because they were Swazis. This would be my second time in South Africa, the second time I would cross a border lawfully. The thought made me happy, but the visa process scared me. I was a refugee, and my father's pockets had holes in them! It would be hard to satisfy the officers' needs.

We were encouraged by David Appel, the admissions counselor at the ALA, to travel together, so we communicated and met in Manzini for our trip to South Africa. It was my first time traveling such a long distance without either my family or a large group of people. I was looking forward to it. We traveled there a week after I had joined St. Marks High School, to start the A-levels. I was still trying to readjust myself to the hostel life, and I was very nostalgic about LIBOSS. But traveling takes all that away, especially when you are visiting a renowned city like Johannesburg and a magnificent institution like the ALA.

Sifiso indicated that he had different travel plans from Swaziland to South Africa, but he would travel back with us. I met Sibonginkhosi at the bus station in Manzini. He wasn't quite the person I was expecting. I had imagined a muscular guy, taller than me and louder. He turned out to be the opposite, and we studied each other as strangers who were soon to be friends. One was a refugee, the other one a Swazi.

We approached the ticket counter and paid, and then we were asked to present our passports and wait in the minibus that was parked in front of the counter. I hesitated for a moment. My passport was the most valuable thing I possessed, knowing very well that it was the only official document (in addition to the non-Swazi Identity card) that I had acquired in a very long time. Some refugees waited a long time to get it, and most never received it at all. Parting with it so casually did not appeal to me. Besides, the conversations and orders to let go of this precious property were being conveyed in siSwati. But I had to let go, and looking at my friend whom we just met parting so freely with his, I followed suit. Then we sat and waited for the Kombi to fill in.

Along the journey, I interacted a little with Sibonginkhosi before we both succeeded in falling asleep. I was reserved, and he was quiet. This combination meant brief interactions, long pauses, and naps. We were in Johannesburg sooner than anticipated; time seemed to speed up, and then our next step was to call the school to send a driver to pick us up. We had to wait for the driver at one of the Gautrain train stations situated in the heart of Johannesburg.

I fell in love with the ALA campus the moment I stepped onto it. I knew I had a whole weekend to explore, but I couldn't contain myself. The moment we were shown to our rooms, I put down my backpack and started walking wherever my legs could take me. We had been told at the reception, that we are not permitted to leave campus without being escorted by one of the security team members, but there was much to see on campus: the amazing library, bigger than any other that I had ever seen; the small classrooms, elegantly arranged with small, individual tables that made an open square; the entertainment hall, so large that my thoughts quickly ran back to LIBOSS and I instantly decided that this was where I belonged; the green pasture, and much more. I was fascinated by every aspect of the school, and I vowed that since I had come here as a finalist, I would leave the place as an admitted student. The future would see to the rest!

In the evening, there was a talent show. I sat in the audience and admired the performances of so many young people doing what they are best at. I wished the Youth Club members were present just for that moment! After the show, I socialized with the other audience members, including two students from the DRC and a Swazi, who were all studying there. They were eager to give me tips on how to prepare for the next day's interview, though I felt a bit uneasy discussing it. I also talked with my fellow finalists who had travelled from Zimbabwe, Lesotho, and within South Africa for the finalist weekend. I was struck by the caliber and the intelligence I witnessed. My evening wasn't complete until I played guitar, apparently surprising those around me, including the admission officer who spotted me gathering a group of ALA students from the corner where he was sitting.

We slept happily but woke up nervous the next morning. We met near the reception, introduced each other in the company of those who were to interview us, received the "ALA finalists" T-shirts, and headed to the building where we would spend the whole day.

Our first task was to present an object we had brought with us. In the email that told us when and how to get to ALA, they had also asked us to bring something that represented us and something we were passionate about. I remembered reading the email, but it had slipped my mind. I had a few seconds to make something up as the others were presenting, so I only listened to those who presented after me. I thought of presenting a song or a poem that I had written along the journey, so I tore a piece of paper from my diary to rewrite it, but then I remembered that it had to be an object. The interpretation would be easy, because I considered myself to be creative enough, but coming up with the thing itself was the difficult part.

I revisited my diary, searching the front pages that I knew had some images, and tore out a page that had a picture of refugee kids running happily down a path with trees in the background and a beautiful scenery in a distance. I stared at it for a short moment, then I had my explanation. I had lived in different refugee camps. Life is miserable in the camps, and people—even young children—are rarely happy. This picture captured one of my passions and strongest desires. I was passionate about nature, which can be seen in the background, and I always desired that which would help make young people, especially young children in the refugee camps, be happy regardless of the dejection, depression, and despondency that their world offered so abundantly. Nature brought me joy, and these kids running happily were surrounded by it. I paused, then everyone stared at me. Yet another spark!

Saturday continued with group activities, tests, individual interviews, and so on. I participated wholeheartedly, knowing that this was my future. I had fallen in love with ALA, and I had no doubt that it, too, had fallen in love with me.

I went back to St. Marks High School and was greeted by exhilarating news. The Form 5 exam results were out, and out of the 1041 students who had sat for the Swaziland/International General Certificate for Secondary Education, I was in the 34th position.

I was among the top ten students in our scaled performances country-wide. A whole new world had opened up.

CHAPTER 7:

DAWN

"No! You can't do such a thing," my father raged. I wasn't sure whether he was scolding me, the system that was to serve me, or the life so full of uncertainties that even in the presence of hope, there was no measure of how much it was. That had been the paradox of our lives. "What madness would that be? Cancel the what? The flight? Don't even …"

"Michael, when are you starting to pack?" my mother interjected, with a slightly different concern. Her voice was agitated, and unlike my father, she seemed to hold tight to the small flames of hope. I had refused to pack, even though it was less than forty-eight hours before my flight out of Swaziland. I had convinced myself that this was the opportunity I had been waiting for, but I struggled so much to continue! Looking back, this could have been despondency, or else the exact opposite of that, whatever that was.

In the few preceding days, I would sit down for a moment, then stand up to grab something from the kitchen. By the time I neared the cooker or the fridge, I would stand for a while, unaware of where I was and what I needed, then go back to the sleeping room or the living room, pick up my guitar, play three chords, put it down, walk outside and back to the kitchen, and so on. I realized that I was getting more and more restless, and I decided to take walks, often with my nieces. I convinced myself that it was a way to bond with them for the last week we were together, but at the same time whenever we were together they occupied my mind enough that it put those frightening thoughts out of my mind. But whether I liked it or not, I *meditated* every time I lay down to take a nap or to sleep.

It always began by looking back at April of the same year, when I received exciting news announcing that I had been awarded the United World Colleges Scholarship, and then a week later that I had been admitted to African Leadership Academy. That was the most intense dilemma that life had ever thrown at me! *Should I choose UWC, where I would get exposure to the entire world in one bubble, or ALA, where I would be with fellow Africans brainstorming solutions to the problems lingering on the continent about which I am so passionate? But what if ... it fails ...* I mean ... getting into South Africa is easy. I can even cross the border ... yes, I can, but the German visa ... what if I choose Germany and I don't get the visa when my place at ALA has been ... *no!*

I would proceed to think about the first instance when my worst fear was realized. I had started applying for the visa, and the Germany embassy rejected my travel document.

Refugee status in Swaziland lasts for only two years before needing renewal. Likewise, the refugee travel document they provide is valid for only two years. I had obtained mine in June 2014, in preparation for the Form 5 class trip to South Africa, after emptying my father's pockets for transportation and missing nearly the whole term of classes. By this time, it was valid for one more year, but I was going to be in Germany for two years. Or at least I hoped to be. The Germans are efficient; they probably looked at the document's expiration date and did not bother looking at the supporting documents. This refusal had resulted in a series of stressful times trying to obtain a new document from the Ministry of Home Affairs. I had been warned that the new document had to be valid for at least three years. Then the drama began, with so many characters, so much time to be wasted, and so little hope to play with.

"Come back tomorrow; today the office is closed."

"Thank you for coming again, but the person in charge of passports has meetings for the whole day. Come back again later."

"I'm really sorry! *Ngiyaxolisa mfana wami!* We can't give you a document that lasts for more than two years. You are a *refugee.*"

"Hello? Koffi on the phone? Please come back next Monday, we will see if we can do something for you. Again, congratulations on this wonderful opportunity."

"Well hmm, the refugee commissioner has agreed. What we can do is to ask the Principal Secretary (P.S.) to make an exception for you. There is no other way. Unfortunately, he is out of the country, so come back next week on Tuesday. I'm very very sorry"

"The P.S. has signed the approval. You will have to go to Office 213 to take a picture for the ID first, because your ID also needs to change."

"Oh, you are here to take the ID picture? And you are from the Refugee Camp? Unfortunately, the system is down today, so we can't help you. Come back tomorrow."

"If you are here for your passport photo, please go downstairs to the first floor and make the payments."

"Now that we are done with the photo, go to the first floor and see the registrar to finalize the other processes, then you can come back on Friday or Monday afternoon to collect your documents."

"Hello? Mr ... Yes sir. I have eh ... (what is your name again?) ... yes, John *my-kaael* who is here for the passport issue. Yes ... it appears that he is below 18 years old, we need an adult who is a relative to him so that he can sign in his name otherwise we can ... *Angekhe sir,* that's not possible! Okay, why don't you call the ... *Make* [siSwati for "Mrs." or "Madam"] ... eh ... Vice Refugee Commissioner so that we discuss the issue? Okay, come *Babe* [siSwati for "Sir." or "Mr."]. *Buya s'towubukha.*"

From the last week of April to the second week of June, this so-called travel document had managed to stretch time, taking longer than forever to become available to me. In the interim, the German consulate had forgotten. Then miraculously, via an official document that was not a passport but was valid for all countries excluding the refugee's country of origin, in my case the DRC, a five-year duration was guaranteed to me. A step forward! I would smile at this stage of my *meditation*, because indeed there was a spark of hope.

My thoughts would then run to one occasion when Mark and Katherine had taken me along on a visit to a US diplomat. The diplomat was straightforward in pointing out that being a refugee and Congolese—I would have preferred to be Congolese before being a refugee—the visa issue would take extra scrutiny. It might take a long time and even be denied. I would think about running to the German consulate in Mbabane, finally making my way to the Germany embassy in Pretoria to take the biometric tests. The only delightful moment there was the hotel I slept in, with a room of my own, a TV for me, a bathroom and toilet, all mine for a night—and of course, the food I bought at restaurant nearby thanks to the money Mark had given me. While in Pretoria, I had walked all the way to the embassy only to be scolded and told that I had to go to the consulate instead because that was where visas were processed. Walking there would have made me miss the appointment, so I decided to take a taxi. The taxi part was a bit irritating to think about, so I would skip that part and focus on the details that mattered: the fact that I had to go through so much trouble to get to Pretoria, and to the German consulate just for my fingers to be photographed by some small, insignificant machine that emitted greenish light.

In my thinking, I would also skip the perseverance that I had shown until this moment, having applied for the Schengen visa the second week of June. It was a day before my flight, the eighteenth of August, 2015, but I still did not have it! The correspondence with the college did not help much, except for boosting my constantly fading faith.

My *meditation*, right before concluding with a deep breath and a long, sorrowful sigh, would then give way to a landscape of uncertainties, unknown possibilities, finally all interrupted by a conversation with my father.

"Look," I told both my father and mother argumentatively, trying to force out my broken and shaky voice. "I have been in touch with the school. They say that it's normal if I don't get the visa now, and they will reschedule the flight to a later time."

"You are not cancelling any flight here! You need to get out of Africa, for the sake of your future." One of them would plead, and I would just stare at them quietly!

I need to get out of Africa! For some reason, these words lingered longer in my mind, but I did not comment on them.

The next morning, I left the house and went to Mbabane. I told my family that I was going there for either of the two reasons: to get the passport with the visa in it and then come back to start packing my few clothes and valuables in preparation for the trip, or to access the Internet so that I could contact the school and kindly ask them to cancel the flight until further notice.

Around a few minutes after 9 a.m. on the twentieth of August, 2015, in a neighbor's van, I sat opposite my nieces. I stared at them, remembering all the joy they have brought to my life, and smiled. They were both five years old and had just started getting used to their uncle going to school—to Mpaka High School where he commuted every day, to St. Marks where he visited almost every month. I stared at them and wondered whether they knew what was happening, whether they understood that they wouldn't see me for a long while. Then I realized that Newton's third law does not only apply to forces—I wouldn't be able to see them for the next nine months either.

My mother, father, sister, and few other family friends were walking to the shopping complex where they would take a *Kombi* to Matsapa. I thought about my mum and wondered how she felt: refugee life had not only taken her far away from all those she cared for but had also separated her from some of her own children. And now she was going to stand and watch her son, her last-born child, leave her just like that! I knew my father was strong, but how would my beloved mother, frail and fragile, take on this emotional trial? Culturally, the last child is meant to stay at home to look after the aging parents while the first-born and all the middle children worked to support the family. But what had the refugee life brought to us? How much loss had we endured? Even besides material loss, the loss of family members and family ties, the loss of kinship and friendship, we were constantly losing our roots. Here I was, about to fly away to a whole new lifestyle and a whole new culture, the terrifying Western culture.

The atmosphere was quite different. Everyone seemed confused: happy to see me heading on a life-altering journey, proud of me for my success, fascinated to see what the future would hold from this family's hero—but then somber and sad that they wouldn't see me in a long time. Perhaps forever, though I had vowed that that would never happen. My father understood, and I assume my mother did too. My sister was different. She was just overjoyed, unlike the rest. My nieces did not understand anything!

We embarked from home, in Khanyisile village, much earlier. The day before, I had called the bus service that operates the Mbabane–King Mswati III International Airport route to inquire about the travel and the times. The advice I got from Mark and Katherine was to be at the airport at least an hour and a half prior to the flight. Then, the driver told me that the bus would leave Mbabane at 11:45 a.m., arriving at King Mswati III International Airport after 1 p.m.

We left the house around 9 a.m. and took a *Kombi* from Malkerns to Matsapha, where we had to wait for the bus. It was when we arrived there that we realized how early we were, and this provoked some uneasiness. Relying solely on the bus was distressing. My mother kept on thinking out loud, "What if the bus does not come?" I understood her concern because they had waited for this day for so long, even if she could not even imagine me leaving her side. To calm her down, I counted for her the number of times I had called the bus driver on the previous day, and recounted the conversation we had had. I even called again, but she insisted that we find a backup plan.

The two hours we waited at Engen station in Matsapha seemed to be a lifetime, longer than the eternity we had spent living as refugees. But besides the bus, I had a slightly different concern. Chatting with my family and playing with my nieces—my kids—made me start to miss them already.

Finally, the bus arrived! It was large and white, with blue inscriptions announcing "KING MSWATI III INTERNATIONAL AIRPORT." It was escorted by two police cars, one in front and the other one behind.

Seeing that inscription reminded me of how we had spent our very first night in the Kingdom of Swaziland sleeping in the corridor between prison cells at Siteki Police Station. And now police officers were escorting me to reach the airport safely in plain daylight. I smiled.

We arrived at the airport at exactly 1 p.m. I was dejected to learn that my family could not get into the inner wing of the airport to see me off, especially my little ones! I would have loved for them to see me board the plane. Maybe they would have understood that I was going far and not coming back any time soon. Maybe it would inscribe on their brains a long-lasting motivation, seeing their uncle fly off.

I tried to linger with my family for as long as I could, but every passing second echoed deep in my brain, communicating that this was the last day, the last hour, the final second. I wanted to stay and be with my family.

I will never forget the hands waving to me unceasingly, and my father's phone camera following each step I took while I climbed the stairs to the boarding platform after I cleared security. My heart told me this was the moment

I had been waiting for. I remembered a line in one of my poems: "When will I find my fled freedom?"

Before the plane took off, I was again seized by mixed feelings of joy and sorrow. But all this was soon forgotten as the plane started off and I felt the thrill of rising into the air, my ears awkwardly reacting to the changes in air pressure while I looked down at the familiar landmarks. For a moment I closed my eyes, and all I could think of was: *I can do all things through Christ who strengthens me. May God's will be done.* For the rest of the flight, I kept thinking about my geography classes, specifically the aerial photographs. It was like I were studying the topography, settlement patterns, and landscapes of Swaziland, and then of South Africa, and then of Africa—my Africa. I wrote songs and poetry.

Mr. Nodder seized my heavily packed suitcase as soon as I descended the stairs of the bus. He might have thought I was very tired after the sixteen-hour flight—my first ever—and more than four hours on a bus from Frankfurt, in addition to the eternal waiting time I endured in the airport. He was so kind. Maybe he thought it wise to receive a fellow from Swaziland by himself. After all, thirteen years working in Waterford Kamhlaba meant a lot to him. It was a lifelong relationship, one comparable to that single belt you own and loop around your waist every time you put on a trouser—new or old. One thing I know for sure is that he is still connected to that wondrous institution.

"Anyone who goes to Robert Bosch College from the Swazi National Committee will have a special place in Mr. Nodder's heart." Jens Walterman, the UWC coordinator, had told me over lunch at Malandela's, a beautiful lodge and restaurant located in Malkerns valley, less than forty kilometers South East of Mbabane, the capital city of Swaziland. Less than six kilometers away from Khanyisile Village, the place where my family lived at the time. It was in late July when I was invited to have lunch with Mr. Jens and a few other special guests, together with few past, present, and future UWC students. The guests had flown in to attend Waterford's Africa Week (the first of its kind there), which we were preparing for then. The theme was "Africa Rising," which had resonated in my imagination, making me think of myself rising too and playing a crucial role in the rise of Africa. Dreams. It was almost a month before I flew to Germany. It had been a privilege to sit with these eminent visitors. I got to know a bit about RBC and UWC in general. I got to argue about scientific and mathematical concepts with people whose brains were much more highly developed than mine, and to taste for the first time some special meals. It pleased me to connect with all the people we met there, to make those contacts. I like having contacts. It makes me feel connected, especially since I was disconnected from my home country—my cherished country. It was a great way of mentally preparing my eager self for taking the leap and starting at UWC.

Together, Mr. Nodder, Jessy (the dog), and I trod triumphantly, if not tiredly, uphill. There was a lot of excitement. Too much to be real. But the time had arrived to meet the whole world in one bubble. The Marshall Islands, Trinidad and Tobago; islands I had never heard of. Kosovo, Bulgaria, Cambodia; countries I never knew existed. Zimbabwe, Syria, the United States of America; the nations that tickled my heart. And more!

So at 4:20 p.m. on August 21, 2015, the day I had worked so hard for, I set foot in UWC Robert Bosch College.

I felt at home. I felt proud, felt a sense of achievement.

I was led into House 6, my new house. There was a green paper hanging on the door with the names of four students and their countries of origin, one familiar: mine. It stared at me, hanging equanimously on the door of Room 102 of House 6.

Everyone was getting their name tags upon arrival, together with a welcome package which consisted of the student handbook, general information about Freiburg and the school, as well as chocolates and other sweets.

Did I want to be called Koffi? Or John? Maybe John Michael—sounded better. We struggled to learn each other's names, students and staff alike. There were a lot of names: simple, compound, complicated, obvious, obscure—quite a large variety.

More than 250 people had instantly entered my life. Not only that, they were a bunch of teenagers, staff members, and others from all over the world. People from at least eighty-eight nations, as I would soon learn. Even though my presence never represented my actual nation, and I spent the entire two years trying to convince myself that I was either a world citizen or simply a confused, helpless, hopeless, homeless character of the world's making. It broke my heart!

Soon, the very first assembly was held. We all gathered in the village square and sat on its semicircular stairs which, under normal circumstances, stared perpetually past the Dreisam River, at the Black Forest on the other side of the valley, had they not been blocked by the student and staff houses, cubes that each hosted up to twenty-six teenagers or the families of two staff members. We all had foreign smiles except for the abundance of Germans; the faces were so diverse. I so enjoyed seeing many young people together, happy and free for a moment from all the misery the world can offer!

Mr. Nodder spoke. And then we were told, to my utter astonishment, that we were not to use "Mum" as a formal way of addressing female adults. And no "Sir" for the male counterparts, either. No dialects or their equivalents. Whether in class or in the students' village square, in the street or in the *Mensa*—the fancy German word for cafeteria.

Jessy remained Jessy. I was John Michael, or whatever I preferred. For me it didn't really matter, for even calling me "Nobody" would have been a true reflection of who I was. But Dr. Kaschiner was Kristin, Mrs. White was Helen, and even Mr. Nodder, the Dumbledore of our Hogwarts, as we were soon to perceive him, transformed: he was Laurence. Not Sir, nor Mr. Nodder, but Laurence. For the rest of my UWC experience, I had to struggle with that! It wasn't the most inspirational thing that had attracted me to UWC, shaped my dreams and gave me *hope*. Yet I had to deal with it.

Nevertheless, I had arrived, this time by my choice.

A new environment. A new beginning. A new adventure.

EPILOGUE:

BLUE HOUR

My time in Europe has been blissful. At times I felt like Deutsche Bahn's best customer, even if my lacking German made me miss a few trains. I have hiked and skied in the tranquil Schwarzwald. I celebrated my 18th birthday in Paris. I strummed my guitar to produce sorrowful melodies inspired by a beautiful silhouette of the Alps rising elegantly behind Lake Geneva in Lausanne. I climbed the peaks of the French Alps while staying in Notre-Dame-de-Bellecombe in Savoie. I was guided through the chambers of the International Criminal Court in The Hague. I trekked Rome, attended mass in the Vatican, and wrote a moving poem inspired by Michelangelo's paintings of the Sistine Chapel. I rested in the touristy Park Güell and tasted new Mediterranean fruits and seafood in Barcelona, then I sweated under the unforgiving summer heat of Madrid while exploring its numerous parks and parishes. If my Western Europe adventures did not fill my memory box, did not satisfy my heart, the three weeks I spent in the *much-feared* United States of America were equally ecstatic.

I like to forget the hardships of obtaining the U.S visa though, and the harassment I got at JFK International Airport because that's what I get at every airport. I mingled with bright peers from many states of the vast country built by immigrants, and from other parts of the world as a Yale Young Global Scholar at Yale University in Connecticut. At the end of the two weeks program I was featured in the YYGS speaker series, and I talked about how we united as youth amid the March 2013 conflicts in Mpaka Refugee Camp. I even performed for them "Should I," (a farewell song I wrote while still at St. Marks High School) before I set to explore New York City and Washington DC with Mark and Katherine.

Being in NYC, just like the first time I visited Amsterdam, I was instantly repelled by the overwhelming crowd. Had I not passed through the Central Park when coming from the Museum of Natural History, heading to St. Patrick's Cathedral, a few streets away from the Trump Tower, I would have eternally thought that there exists no air to breathe in NYC. I couldn't help but wonder how pedestrians, and the homeless seemed so miniature and so inferior in the shadows of the tall sky scrapers, and the people of color appeared like ants navigating a giant anthill. I enjoyed walking through the less busy streets of Lower Manhattan and World Trade Center.

My highlight was the moving guided tour of the United Nations Headquarters we had before taking a ferry to see the Statue of Liberty, and eventually leaving for DC.

Mark and Katherine ensured I had an optimum experience of both renowned cities. While in DC, a guided tour of the U.S Capitol and its surrounding had been organized. Walking in DC felt like walking on the Palatine Hill in Rome. We visited the Holocaust Museum, and horrified, I swallowed my tears and suppressed my anger, just as I had done when I visited the Jewish Museum in Berlin a few months earlier. My joy was later roused by standing on the Lincoln Memorial steps, thinking of the famous "I have a Dream" speech by Martin Luther King Jr. I had a great time.

If I ever forget all these memories, there is one image I will forever hold on tightly: Sitting at a harbor across the Hudson River in Jersey City, looking at how the tall towers of NYC unwillingly reflected the golden rays of the sunset. The reflection sent me into a trance, and my eyes went awash – an uncontrollable emotion I had never had before. At the back of my mind I was wondering, "what have I ever done to be here? Who could have ever thought I would be here? *A refugee?*" And then I thought of all the struggles of young people in the refugee camps. I thought of the exhibition at the UN headquarters which featured stories of the refugees from the DRC into South Sudan, and from South Sudan into the DRC, along with "Clouds Over Sidra," a short 3D virtual reality documentary of a twelve-year-old Syrian girl living in Zaatari refugee camp in Jordan. I thought about my shadowy past and my uncertain future, then I stared at the reflection of the sunset from the NYC skyscrapers. I wondered why I had lived to see that day.

Close to the Blue Hour, I rejoined Mark and Katherine inside DoubleTree hotel and did not say a word. I would soon have one more guided tour at Georgetown University, and then head back to Germany.

In the past few months, as I neared the end of my time in Freiburg, I was admitted to two world-class universities: Georgetown University in Washington, DC and the University of British Columbia in Vancouver. I did not complete any other university applications.

I had to make a choice similar to when I had to choose between the African Leadership Academy and the United World College. I looked at my travel document: it would expire in 2020, in three years. My heart beat faster and unevenly, a reaction to the hassle endured to get this single most important piece of paper. I was in no mood to reenact the same drama with the Swazi officials three years later, but would either the United States or Canada be an escape route? I would be doing a four-year-long degree or more at either of the two universities; either I would get a tangible paper or I would still be a refugee.

I thought of the new scandal that happened to the US and heeded the general opinion. Canada would be the place! At least the ripple effect of the US presidential orders, its Islamophobia, and its anti-refugee sentiment wouldn't affect my visa application. But I would think, "UBC is great. I am an International Leader of Tomorrow, and I'm glad they recognized that! But the Arrupe scholarship was generous too, and Georgetown is the best for law and international relations. Although I don't want to be a politician—politics stinks. But DC would have more opportunities—and ... crap, my travel document!"

I rejected Georgetown—my top choice university. I accepted UBC's admissions offer and embarked on the study permit application journey.

I started the application on the twenty-sixth of April, 2017. "The applications of those applying from Germany are processed within two weeks," the official Canadian Immigration website said. The website emphasized that the notice was "updated weekly."

I waited for two weeks—no response. The third week kicked in. The fourth arrived, and I sent an inquiry that got me no response. The fifth week, I received an update. I had to pay the biometrics fee. "Payment received." Another notification. I had to go to the nearest Visa Application Centre (VAC) to get my biometrics taken. Dusseldorf it was, and then it would be done! I lied to myself.

What efficiency! Within three minutes of my arrival at the VAC, they were done helping me. I came back to Freiburg and waited one more week. Six weeks in total, and I had already forgotten that "the applications of those applying from Germany are processed within two weeks."

Six weeks after my application was submitted online and received, the verdict came in. It turned out that I was still a refugee: "After a careful review of your study permit application and supporting documentation, I have determined that your application does not meet the requirements of the Immigration and Refugee Protection Act and Regulations. I am refusing your application."

It was a dagger to the heart. My faith was crushed. I read it again, checked the date and the application number to make sure it was meant for me. I reread the sentence and the reasons. I reread again, and again, and every time I read "I am refusing your application," the dagger thrust deeper and deeper. Since I had my verdict, I had to know the reason why I was rejected, at least. After all, I was only guilty of being a refugee who wanted to pursue his education and change his family's situation. One who wanted an amazing opportunity in a Western country in order to change, hopefully, the situation that his family and he had been running away from for the past nearly eight years. A situation that had claimed many, decapitated many others, and could only get worse!

"You have not satisfied me that you would leave Canada at the end of your stay."

Seriously? The dagger reached the core. Canada. I felt lost for words in disbelief, wondering where next my crime would take me if this were not an option. Maybe I was wrong about the presidential orders. They were everywhere. I communicated with RBC, my friends in Germany, and UBC in Canada. My teachers engaged some lawyers, all of whom came to one conclusion: I would have to reapply and *hope*.

It is exactly two weeks and two days after I submitted a new application. I am still applying from Germany, where "the applications of those applying from Germany are processed within two weeks."

It is July 12, 2017, a little after five o'clock in the afternoon. I am sitting on top of artificial rocks at the bank of the Pegnitz river, close to Ebenseesteg in Nuremberg, Germany. It is raining, and the clouds seem pregnant as they eagerly hinder the sunrays from trespassing their colonies. I wish I was small, the little fella who ran on top of hills and at the bottom of valleys, playing with the droplets decelerated by tree leaves in the *safe* parts of the forests. But I can't! I am alone and lonely. Do I just go to sleep, with a troubled mind and restless spirit?

ACKNOWLEDGMENTS

All thanks to my parents, and my brothers and sisters, for their unconditional love and support, for encouraging me to aim higher, and in this case for unknowingly giving me memory cues for different sections of the book. Thanks to "my" Youth Club in Swaziland, and all my friends in the refugee camps for their inspiration, and permission to give a glimpse of the stories we share. In particular, I think of Alberto and Christian (whose paths crossed mine in both Malawi and Swaziland and remain closer to my heart than any peer I know), Sophia and her family, as well as Sandra and her family. I am also grateful to the people in the Ministry of Home Affairs in Swaziland who have supported my education and zeal to succeed against all odds. This achievement would not have been possible without the support they gave me, my family, and other refugees in Mpaka. To the alumni and students of Waterford Kamhlaba (WK) who were/are part of the Mpaka Community Service, your encouraging words and deeds will forever be remembered by the many young refugees in Mpaka whose lives you (have) touch(ed). And that includes me whom you have told about United World Colleges (UWC) and African Leadership Academy (ALA)—the two institutions that have significantly shaped my ideology and pan-Africanism.

My humble gratitude to the UWC community. I thank the Swazi UWC National Committee, especially John Storer at WK. This book is a testimony of the opportunities you have given, and you continue to give the refugees in Mpaka. Thanks to Jacqueline Borgstedt (UWC Robert Bosch College class of 2016) for caring so much about the refugees and initiating the meeting that ignited the spark in me to write this book. To Colin Habgood and Jill Longson (UWC Atlantic College, class of 1981) and your GoMakeADifference (GoMAD) grant team; after the uplifting and directive sentiments from the UWC RBC community, being awarded the GoMAd grant was another remarkable driving force to write *Refuge-e: The Journey Much Desired,* and for this I will be forever grateful. Thanks to all my RBC teachers and staff members for their encouragement, lifelong lessons, and support. In particular, I thank my English teachers and personal tutors. Thanks to Hubertus Zander—the admissions and university counselor whose wisdom informs and shapes future aspects of many, if not all, RBC graduates— and Kristin Kaschner, my biology teacher, an Environmental Laureate whose love I embrace as a son. To Laurence Nodder, the Rector of UWC RBC and former Principal of WK, and your wife Debbie Nodder, teacher at UWC RBC and former coordinator of WK's Mpaka Community Service during your time in

Swaziland, I'm blessed to have been under your guidance and care during my time in Germany, and to know how much you believe in me and want me to succeed.

Lasting gratitude to you Mark and Katherine Fulford for your unreserved support for my education, for reorienting some of my ideas in this memoir, and, importantly, for being my second family. Thanks to you Klaus and Ute Steger for supporting me, accepting me as your own, showing me so much love, and reassuring me that there is a brighter future—be it through *the* book or through my persistence and positive attitude to life.

Lastly, I am indebted to Kenneth Wee and Michael Grathwohl, my copyeditors, who worked diligently to give life to my still developing command of the English language, and to Matt Begg and Brittani Todson at Tellwell Talent for working with me to get this work published.

O! What a world we long to see!